MUSIC IN WORDS

MUSIC IN WORDS

A Guide to Researching and
Writing about Music

Trevor Herbert

The Associated Board of the Royal Schools of Music

First published in 2001 by
The Associated Board of the Royal Schools of Music (Publishing) Limited
24 Portland Place, London W1B 1LU, United Kingdom

Reprinted in 2003

ISBN 1 86096 236 X

AB 2792

Design and formatting by Geoffrey Wadsley
Printed in England by Alden Group Limited, Oxford

Illustration acknowledgements
Fig. 3.2 BLPC Internet search screen, reproduced by kind permission of The British Library. Fig. 3.3 The Open University Internet search screen, reproduced by kind permission. Fig. 5.3 Extract from *The New Langwill Index*, reproduced by kind permission. Fig. 5.6 Extract from Robert Philip: *Early Recordings and Musical Style*, © 1992 Cambridge University Press, reproduced by kind permission. Fig. 5.8 Illustration reproduced by permission of La Bibliothèque Historique de la Ville de Paris. Caption taken from the entry for 'Grand opéra' in *The New Grove Dictionary of Music and Musicians*, 2nd edn, © 2001 Macmillan Publishers Ltd, reproduced by kind permission. Fig. 5.9 Table from Cyril Ehrlich: *The Piano: A History*, © 1990 Oxford University Press, reproduced by kind permission. Fig. 5.10 Table taken from the entry for 'Orchestra' in *The New Grove Dictionary of Music and Musicians*, © 1980 Macmillan Publishers Ltd, reproduced by kind permission. Fig. 5.11 Title page from Matthew Locke: *Little Consort of Three parts, 'Treble and Tenor'*, 1656, reference (shelf-mark) Wood 278, reproduced by permission of the Bodleian Library, University of Oxford. Table 7.1 Table of abbreviations for instruments and voices taken from *Guidelines for Contributors* for *The New Grove Dictionary of Music and Musicians*, 2nd edn, © 1995 Macmillan Publishers Ltd, reproduced by kind permission. Fig. 8.1 Definition of 'violin' reproduced from the *Oxford English Dictionary Online*, © 1989 & 2001 Oxford University Press, reproduced by permission. Fig. 8.2 Extract from the entry for 'Rondo' in *The New Grove Dictionary of Music and Musicians*, 2nd edn, © 2001 Macmillan Publishers Ltd, reproduced by kind permission. Fig. 8.3 Extract from the entry for 'John Philip Sousa' in *The New Grove Dictionary of Music and Musicians*, 2nd edn, © 2001 Macmillan Publishers Ltd, reproduced by kind permission. Fig. 8.4 Extract from the work-list in the entry for 'Ludwig van Beethoven' in *The New Grove Dictionary of Music and Musicians*, 2nd edn, © 2001 Macmillan Publishers Ltd, reproduced by kind permission. Fig. 8.5 Extracts from Vincent Duckles: *Music Reference and Research Materials: An Annotated Bibliography*, 5th edn, © 1997 Schirmer Books, reproduced by permission.

Front cover music extract from Philip Cashian: *Landscape*, included in *Spectrum*, © 1996 by The Associated Board of the Royal Schools of Music.

CONTENTS

ACKNOWLEDGEMENTS

This is a short book and, on the face of it, a fairly straightforward one; but the writing of it proved to be more troublesome and perplexing than I had anticipated. Two problems always loomed large: the possibility that what seemed clear to me would be considerably less clear to anyone else; and the inevitable danger that I overlook one of the devices or regulations of which I emphasize the importance in this book. The primary device I used for limiting such dangers was to ask several people to read the material for me. I tested the limits of friendship by persuading people whose clarity of thought I admire to read either part or all of the first draft and to offer me their comments. These included Pam Barlow, Trevor Bray, Donald Burrows, Stew Carter, Aled Herbert, Alexander McGrattan, Jeff Nussbaum, Keith Polk and John Wallace. Trevor Bray also read a revised draft and picked up a number of points that I had missed. The comments I received from these highly qualified people were invaluable to me.

I am also indebted to the staff of ABRSM (Publishing) Ltd, especially Philip Croydon, as well as to Judith Nagley for copy-editing the text. I want particularly to record my gratitude to Caroline Perkins, who has managed the production of this book calmly, helpfully and with great efficiency.

My greatest debt is to Helen Barlow, who has worked with me from the start of this project. She deserves much of any credit that is due for the clarity and accuracy of many parts of the book that deal with generic matters about writing. But her greatest contribution was to remind me regularly of the virtue of plain common sense.

However, I must make it clear that I have not accepted the advice of any of the above-mentioned wholesale. Consequently, any errors, omissions or points of confusion that remain can be attributed only to me.

Trevor Herbert
Cardiff 2001

A NOTE ABOUT ACADEMIC WRITING CONVENTIONS

Anyone with a modest familiarity with academic writing conventions will know that they are not totally standardized – especially where musical matters are concerned. Despite the fact that so many different styles and conventions co-exist (a point I reiterate several times), this book contains clear advice about how things should be done. So how have I decided what should or should not be written?

- In most cases, I have not suggested a rule as the only correct one. Where more than one way of doing something is widely acceptable, I have said so. My intention has not been to provide a list of definitive rules, but rather to give a collection of *legitimate* conventions that, if used consistently, can form a perfectly good basis for writing about music.
- I have decided what is legitimate by scrutinizing three different types of source:
  1. Style manuals such as *The Chicago Manual of Style*, 14th edn (University of Chicago Press, 1993); Judith Butcher's *Copy-Editing: The Cambridge Handbook for Editors, Authors and Publishers*, 3rd edn (Cambridge University Press, 1992); the *MHRA Style Book*, 5th edn (London: The Modern Humanities Research Association, 1996); and D. Kern Holoman's *Writing about Music: A Style Sheet from the Editors of 19th-Century Music* (Berkeley: University of California Press, 1988).
  2. The house-style sheets of major publishers who have published some of my own work – these include Oxford University Press, Cambridge University Press, Macmillan (the publishers of Grove's dictionaries and encyclopedias) and some USA-based publishing houses.
  3. Several specific publications about music. I have taken some

care to observe custom and practice by looking at well-respected publications from different areas of scholarship. These include academic journals and monographs. I have paid particular attention to the conventions used in *The New Grove Dictionary of Music and Musicians*, 2nd edn (2001) (*New Grove II*), and also to the styles and formats used in the ABRSM's own publications.

- From this, I have attempted to find a broad agreement about the way things might be done. Where no such consensus appears to exist, I have made a subjective and pragmatic judgement based on what I see as the clearest, simplest and least fussy solution to a particular problem.

- There is, however, one matter that has required special attention. It concerns the way that sources such as books are acknowledged in academic writing. Two main methods exist: the author–date system, and the short-title system. These two systems are equally favoured, and they are so fundamental to scholarly writing that I have provided an explanation of both.

It is abundantly clear that many legitimate conventions co-exist, and no claim is made that the procedures suggested here are the best. My intention is simply to encourage you to be aware of the alternatives that are favoured by some other writers.

I have used a number of book titles and pieces of text to illustrate the conventions I discuss. Some of the titles are real, but others are not; and all the textual 'extracts' are manufactured in order to demonstrate the use of citation methods and so on.

INTRODUCTION

This book is about the way we research music and write about it. Throughout, the emphasis is on the practicalities of doing this, and as such it is no less practical than any other book published by the ABRSM. The aim is to provide an introductory explanation of how to investigate or research music efficiently, and write about it in a way that does good research proper credit. It is not a comprehensive guide; rather, it is an introduction and a compendium of information – a textbook and a brief reference manual. But why is such a book needed, and why is it published by the world's largest examiner of musical performance?

Most music students need to study and write about music as part of a broad musical education. Those who are serious about this want to do it well, and to do it well they need appropriate skills. But students and examination candidates are not the only people who can benefit from practical guidance in researching and writing. Increasingly, performers are contributing to literature about music. Some write books and articles, and many more compile their own concert programme and CD liner notes. This is the way it should be; performers gain a special intimacy with repertoire and performance techniques, and are authorities in their specialism. But when musicians are confronted with the need to find reliable information and then put pen to paper, the task can appear daunting. What makes good researchers work effectively, and how do the techniques and conventions of writing work? Indeed, why are there conventions at all? Why do academic writings look different and have a different tone from some other forms of literature?

People can be gifted writers in the same way as others are gifted pianists. But every performer knows that there are performance skills to be learned, and those skills are based on a shared understanding of what constitutes a good technique. There is an analogy here with the rules and conventions that apply to writing. Performers do not just learn how to play or sing; they learn how to do it properly, but at the same time they retain an expression of their individuality in the way they perform. This is reflected in writing too: we use the rules and conventions as a framework for expressing our ideas about music. The rules or conventions of academic writing help ensure that our meaning comes across clearly.

Why write about music?

Musicians need to understand music as well as perform it, because performers, composers and educators are not merely executants: they are interpreters too. To interpret, we have not only to probe deeply into the music we perform, but also to look further and wider than the music itself. Music has to be understood from several perspectives. We gain such understanding by studying music theory, individual works, repertoires, instruments, performance practices, the biographies of composers, national cultures and many other topics. But if musical knowledge is to be purposeful and invigorating, it must be refreshed by the ideas that derive from a constant discourse about music. At the highest levels this discourse takes the form of scholarly debates and publications. Performers are involved in this discourse – indeed, much of it is about repertoire and performance practice. But it is not just in academic journals that musical discourse has an impact. Every magazine article and programme or CD liner note carries information and ideas, and these writings engage the listening public, heightening their understanding and enjoyment of music.

Why research?

'Research' can be an intimidating word. It suggests a level of investigation that is the preserve of professional academics. This is not the case, and throughout this book I have used the word consistently to mean methodical or systematic investigation as opposed to a more casual and arbitrary approach. All musicians need to have basic research skills so that they can obtain information efficiently and recognize the difference between reliable and unreliable material. Even the simplest task – finding music or basic information about a composer – can be more difficult than it need be if you are unsure of your starting point. I make a distinction in this book between short and longer, more ambitious research projects, but it is worth examining some of the ideas I suggest for longer research projects, no matter how modest your intentions are.

What the book aims to do

This book does not provide recipes for every type of writing task or for every research project. At each stage and in each section, it introduces you to methods and procedures that enable and encourage you to find your own way. It provides hints about how to get started with a research project, how to write, how to organize your writing and how to observe some of the basic academic writing conventions such as footnotes and bibliographies. But if you want more detail on any of these topics, you will have to follow up some of the further reading suggestions given at the end of each chapter.

How the book works

This is both a textbook and a reference book, and for this reason it is in two parts, even though the chapters are numbered sequentially. Part I provides advice on how to research and write; Part II is a compendium of information. The following devices in particular are intended to make the book clear and useful:
- Cross-references (for example 'See also "Performance directions" on page X') are given if significantly more information on the topic you are looking at can be found elsewhere in the book.
- The glossary, which appears towards the end of the book, gives brief explanations of technical words (other than musical terms, for which see Chapter 7). Many of these words are used in the book, but others are additional terms that you may come across in your other reading. This section too is cross-referenced.
- A brief bibliography is given at the end of each chapter, containing a selection of useful books and World Wide Web sites that are relevant to the subject of that chapter.
- An index is given at the end of the book, in which topics are usually listed under several different words so that you stand a better chance of finding what you are looking for.
- References are given to World Wide Web sites – especially in the bibliographies and in Chapters 3 and 8. These sites are susceptible

to change, and new sites are being launched continually. To cope with this, the ABRSM has set up a *Music in Words* Web page that can be accessed through the ABRSM (Publishing) Ltd site <http://www.abrsmpublishing.co.uk/musicinwords>. It contains hypertext links to all sites mentioned in this book, and a great many more.

Part I

Chapter one

HOW TO WRITE: SOME BASICS FOR SHORTER WRITING TASKS

T HE PURPOSE of this chapter is twofold: to give some basic advice on how to approach writing tasks, and to provide suggestions for specific shorter writing projects. Throughout, the emphasis is on the importance of clarity and straightforwardness in writing, and on offering some guidance on how to achieve this.

The chapter deals with the following issues:

- why writing is different from speaking;
- different types of writing: finding the right content, form and style;
- some questions to ask when writing about musical works;
- writing essays;
- writing in examinations;
- writing CD liner notes;
- writing concert programme notes;
- writing reviews;
- writing for reading aloud.

For advice on aspects of language usage, see Chapter 6.

Why writing is different from speaking

One of the basic problems encountered by inexperienced writers is in understanding and accommodating the difference between spoken and written language. *Spoken* language is full of colloquialisms and incomplete sentences, and there are times when writers of dialogue (novelists, playwrights or screenwriters, for instance) need to write in a way that imitates this. Indeed, although the language of speeches and scholarly papers is much more formal than conversational language, most people delivering a speech or paper feel the need to make it sound less formal than written language. But when you speak you have a range of additional ways of communicating your meaning – your intonations, expressions and gestures convey important nuances, and these ensure that you convey your meaning accurately. Even in written communications there are different levels of formality, and these different levels arise because there is a need for them. Personal or informal writing, such as e-mail messages or letters, is different from academic writing. In such informal modes, you can often rely on the person or people you are addressing knowing you, and understanding the way you think, your sense of humour and so on.

Academic writing requires you to take more care with the language that you use, but this is not for the sake of mere formality and pedantry. In fact, you should avoid using over-elaborate sentences, or choosing words merely because you think they sound impressive or intellectual. Rather, academic language places emphasis on correctness and precision in order to ensure that information is conveyed accurately and that ideas are accessible and unambiguous. Good academic writing is writing that takes account of the needs of both the writer and the reader. It requires you to consider the following issues:

- In most cases (books, articles, theses, dissertations, for instance), your work will be read by readers whom you do not know, and who do not know you. (Even if it is to be marked by a tutor who knows you well, you should write as though your work will be read by readers whom you do not know, because an essay is a training exercise in the use of academic language.)
- The ideas you want to communicate are likely to be more complex and detailed than any you would discuss in conversation or in an e-mail, for example.
- Your work may be read by specialists, but it may also be read by people with a less detailed or sophisticated knowledge of the subject than you.
- Your work may be read by people whose first language is not the same as the language you have written in.

For all these reasons, your central concern must be to communicate your ideas clearly and without ambiguity. Once your essay or thesis is submitted, or your article, book or programme notes are handed over to the publisher or printer, you have only your written words to rely on for this; so you must be sure that you have written in a way that will be clear and unambiguous.

People often make the mistake of writing in a self-conscious style, using long, over-complicated words and sentences – usually because they feel insecure and inexperienced as writers, and want to appear impressive, or to mimic the style of others whom they admire and consider to be experts. Your sentences will be all the clearer for being as short and direct as possible, and you should avoid words that merely *sound* clever, as well as those that are slangy and colloquial (and thus might not be understood by some readers). Do not worry that you may be writing in too straightforward a style.

You should also think about the clearest and most effective way to structure your ideas – another common mistake is to plunge straight into writing, trying to write down your ideas right away in seamless prose, without giving thought to the structure of the piece. You may have very clear views on the issue in question, but you may *not* have considered how best to construct a convincing and interesting way of expressing them.

Different types of writing: finding the right content, form and style

Content, form and style are the three elements that constitute a piece of writing. The *content* (as the word implies) is the substance that is contained in it. *Form* (or structure) is the way that the writing is ordered and laid out, and the *style* is the tone, the manner of address. In academic writing there is a legitimate need to use certain formal procedures and these are described elsewhere in this book. But formal academic writing is not the only type of writing that musicians engage with. Neither does it have a monopoly over intelligent, stimulating and important literature about music. Later in this book I explain why formal academic writing conventions are used, but it is important to stress that there are other modes of writing for which such conventions are unnecessary and inappropriate.

Popular writings about music – those contained in popular books, magazines and programme and CD liner notes, for example – account for a large proportion of literature about music. This type of literature is hugely important to musical discourse because it reaches such a wide audience. It informs the people who make up the audience for live and recorded music. This audience has exacting standards and requires literature that is no less engaging, authoritative and accurate than music academics and students require. It is neither necessary nor appropriate to use formal academic conventions in popular writings. But it is important to stress that more popular (or, should I say, less formal) writings are not form*less*. It is simply that, because their content is different from academic writing (shorter, less detailed and aimed at the non-specialist reader), they require a different approach so that the ideas can be conveyed in a way that is clear, accessible and attractive to the readership.

Writers use different styles in recognition of the different functions or purposes of particular pieces of writing. The wide range of publications about music provides evidence of this diversity. Academic essays, dissertations and theses are the main species of writing that students are involved with. Essays (sometimes they are called projects) are usually relatively short pieces, anything from about 1,000 to 5,000 words. As a rule, essays are written in response to a given question or rubric. Dissertations and theses – the two words are often used synonymously – are much longer works (a PhD thesis could be up to 100,000 words long, the Fellowship of the Royal Schools of Music (FRSM) diploma sometimes requires a 12,000-word submission). For dissertations and theses there is an absolute requirement that all the necessary academic conventions are used. Indeed the accuracy with which these conventions are applied is one of the main things that examiners look for. While the full paraphernalia of academic conventions are unnecessary for shorter essays, it is worth trying to understand these conventions, because many of the books that you are likely to consult use them: anyone with a serious interest in musical discourse should know what they mean. Further to this there are other factors that are as common to essay writing as they are to more advanced projects. These include the need for accuracy, clarity and the ability to be able to find reliable information about music easily.

Writing for a non-academic readership can be daunting. Music can be one of the most difficult things to write about, because there are unique challenges. The subject can be complex; to understand it fully we have to understand notation, rhythm, harmony, formal structures, musical styles and idioms, biographies, histories, instruments, audiences – the list could go on. But at the heart of all musical discourse is the music itself: an art form that is primarily intended to be *heard*. When we write about music, the subject that we write about – the music itself – is absent. Multimedia, on-line publications offer the prospect of moving instantly between written text, pictures and sounds, but in the medium that this book is mainly about – the written word – readers have to imagine or remember the music that is being referred to.

We can of course provide written music quotations, and if you are writing for a musically literate audience, this is fine. Indeed in some types of writing – writings centred on musical analysis, for example – notated music allows scrutiny of music scores at a level of detail that writers on some other subjects envy. I deal with the incorporation of notated music into text more than once in the course of this book. But it is worth remembering that most people cannot read music; to them, notated music means absolutely nothing. It therefore follows that there are many types of popular writing for which music quotations are inappropriate. I have often wondered how many members of an average concert audience appreciate being confronted with an analysis of the work they are about to hear, richly illustrated with notated music, in the five or ten minutes between buying a programme and the start of the concert.

The basic points to emphasize about content, form and style are that:

- Your writing must be fit for its purpose: its *content, form* and *style* must serve the needs of your intended readership.
- Irrespective of those aspects of style that distinguish your writing from that of others, your writing must be clear: it must be so clear that everyone who reads it takes from it only the meaning that you wish to convey.
- What you write must be founded on a clear and accurate under-standing of your subject. This means that you have to know where to find reliable and authoritative information about music.

Some questions to ask when writing about musical works

It is impossible to anticipate the many reasons why you would want to write about a particular piece of music. However, my intention here is to list some of the issues that you might address when looking at a music score or an extract from a score. Some of the points mentioned here could make a checklist for examination questions that require a brief essay about a piece of music. My list is biased towards interpre-tation and performance. It would be considerably longer if it embraced, for example, wider aspects of musicology or pedagogy. I

suggest that you think about two aspects of any given work:
- issues concerning its musical nature – its structure and musical language;
- issues about its context, especially those that might influence its interpretation and performance.

Some points may seem a little too self-evident, but they are all important. I should also stress that you should not think of a piece of music as a collection of details. The most important impression you should establish about any musical work concerns its total effect: the way its structure and other elements combine to make it coherent and expressive. Detailed comments can give substance to that impression, and matters of context also inform our understanding of the work. You will notice that some of these questions relate very closely to each other. Not all of them will necessarily be relevant to your needs, but the list should stimulate you into thinking about other specific aspects of the work.

Questions to ask about the structure and formal elements

- Is the work a complete or self-contained piece, or is it an extract from a larger work or series of pieces? Does this have a bearing on its structure?
- What are the instrumental and/or vocal forces that the work is written for? Are these forces typical or unusual in works of this type?
- Where are the main musical 'landmarks' in the piece (the places that seem to mark important structural or expressive points), and what makes them prominent?
- What are the formal or structural characteristics of the piece? How do these structures work? (In tonal music you will almost certainly be looking at harmonic progressions and key changes.) Do they follow a particular formal pattern, such as sonata form or rondo?
- What can be said about the harmonic language of the piece? Is it diatonic, predominantly chromatic or atonal?
- What textures are used? Is the texture contrapuntal or homophonic? ('Homophonic' could mean melody/accompaniment or chordal texture.)
- Does rhythmic or metrical complexity seem prominent?

- What are the prominent melodic phrases?
- Are contrasts and/or repetitions prominent?
- Is there any borrowed material in the work (such as themes or music quotations)? Does the composer draw on a borrowed framework (such as a much earlier form) or on some other material or ideas?
- How is mood conveyed, and is there just one mood throughout the piece or does it change?
- If the work is vocal, does the composer try to express the meaning of individual words or phrases in the music?
- If there are words, who wrote them and in what language? Is the setting you are examining in the original language?
- Are the instruments or voices used idiomatically – that is, are they used in a way that shows an awareness of their special characteristics and techniques? Are wide tessituras used for solo voices or instruments?
- Are the performance directions (if there are any) distinctive in any way? Are dynamics and tempo changes frequent?

Questions to ask about compositional and performance context

- Who wrote the work, and when and where was it first performed?
- Why was it written (perhaps for particular performers, or as a commission)? Is the music functional (dance or ceremonial music, for example)?
- Did the composer complete the work, or was it completed by someone else?
- Did the composer revise the work?
- Was it published during the composer's lifetime?
- Is the edition you are looking at the original version or a later edition?
- At what point in the composer's life and output was the piece written? Does it relate to or contrast with other pieces written at about the same time? How does it fit into the general creative output of the composer?
- Are there extra-musical factors concerning the composer's life that might be reflected in the piece?
- Does the title have significance? Is it just the name of a genre (sonata or concerto, for instance), or is the title more descriptive?

Is the work programmatic – is it supposed to portray or evoke events and characters?

- How detailed are the performance instructions? Are the performance forces (names and quantities of instruments/voices) given? Are dynamics, tempi, accidentals and ornamentation specified? How much discretion is given to performers? Are they expected to understand unwritten conventions such as ornamentation?
- What was the reception of the work when it was first heard? Have there been different attitudes to or receptions of the piece subsequently?
- How or where does the work fit into a broad historical context? Does it respond to or reflect broad cultural or historical movements or events?
- How does the work fit into the development of repertoire for the forces (instruments, voices) for which it was written?

Writing essays

The essay is one of the first types of writing that people encounter. It is therefore a good starting point for explaining the process of writing. This process involves:
- making sure you understand the question;
- planning your response to it;
- finding the information that will be put into the essay;
- drafting the essay;
- refining it;
- checking it.

As you can see, writing up the final version of the essay comes late in the process. It is the stage you reach when you are sure that the overall structure and flow of your argument works. (This may sound like an over-simplification where long works such as dissertations are concerned, but it is not. It is simply that here 'writing up' is something that you are most likely to do a section or chapter at a time, rather than treating it as a continuous task and working through from beginning to end as you might do with a short essay.)

There are five main stages that need to be worked through before you think of setting your ideas on paper in their final form.

1 Answering questions

Most academic essays require you to answer questions that have been set for you. Questions are not merely tests; they are the means by which teachers train students to think about music, to formulate ideas about it and to articulate those ideas through writing. I suggest in Chapter 2 that one of the best ways of developing a more ambitious research project, one for which you have selected the title yourself, is to ask questions about it. This basic idea of formulating questions to help develop your thoughts is one that recurs throughout this book. A good way to start is by looking at how you might address an essay question.

Think about the title of your piece, or the essay question you have been set. What does it require you to do? How many words are you allowed in which to do it? What are the 'keywords' (or phrases) of the title or question?

Consider the following essay title:

'Discuss whether Beethoven's creative output can be divided into three clearly defined periods.'

Obvious keywords and phrases are:
- *Beethoven*, as this identifies the figure who is the central focus of the essay;
- *three clearly defined periods*, as this identifies the particular aspect of Beethoven's work you need to address.

You should also think very carefully about the word or words that identify the particular task that you have been set. In this instance, the task is to *discuss whether*. This means that you are being asked to *give the reasons for and against* thinking of Beethoven's creative output as falling into three periods.

If the question asked you to ***Explain why Beethoven's creative output can be divided into three clearly defined periods***, it would be asking you to do something else: to give the reasons *for* thinking of Beethoven's work in this way. Words like 'discuss' and 'explain' are called the 'process words' of an essay question. The process words are always keywords when it comes to considering exactly what you are being asked to do.

2 Planning

You will have done some reading around your subject before you reach this stage, but it is important to have a preliminary plan of the structure of the essay, and to have drawn some provisional conclusions, before you start doing any specific research for your piece – that is, looking for material and taking notes from it. You will probably want to rethink the plan once you have gathered your material, but having an initial plan is helpful in establishing where to start your research. A plan sets out the issues you feel you need to cover in order to lead your reader from the title or question to your conclusion about it, and this helps you in determining what in particular you need to investigate, and what books and articles you need to find to do so.

You cannot plan effectively unless you know, at least roughly, what your answer or conclusion is, and you cannot know this unless you understand what the question or title requires of you. So be sure that you have properly worked through stage 1 above.

Having established a provisional conclusion, you should consider carefully what points you will need to make in order to lead your reader logically and persuasively from the question or title to your conclusion. These points will form the main body of your essay. Put them down on paper in the order in which you think you will probably need to tackle them, so as to create a progression of ideas; and leave plenty of space around them, so that you can make amendments and add notes and reminders to yourself. Taking the example we used in stage 1, your provisional plan might look like Fig. 1.1 opposite.

You now have a basis for stage 3, but remember that this is only a provisional plan, so you should reconsider it, and if necessary rework it, before you start on stage 4.

3 Researching

When you prepare a short academic essay, your research will be limited and defined by the course you are studying. You probably will not need to look much further for your material than the curriculum that you have been taught and relevant entries in *The New Grove Dictionary of Music and Musicians,* 2nd edn (*New Grove II*) or one of the shorter reference or textbooks. However, if you are interested in the process of researching, you might dip into Chapter 2 'Doing

'Discuss whether Beethoven's creative output can be divided into three clearly defined periods.'

PLAN

(1) Introduction
    i. Long tradition of thinking of 3 periods (give egs)
    ii. <u>But</u> the 3-period idea has been challenged
    iii. All periodizations should be treated with caution

(2) Period 1
    i. Define period - mention possibility of division into 2 'early' periods to include early (Bonn) works
    ii. Characteristics of period/s
    iii. Illustration
    iv. Works that might not fit into the period

(3) Period 2
    i. Define period (traditional dates) - suggest subdivision
    ii. Characteristics of period
    iii. Illustration
    iv. Works that might not fit into the period

(4) Period 3
    i. Define period (traditional dates)
    ii. Characteristics of period
    iii. Illustration
    iv. Works that might not fit into the period

(5) Conclusion
    i. Brief summary - broad periodization can be helpful if used with caution
    ii. A 3-period model is still helpful, but - as <u>New Grove</u> says - it needs 'some refining' to take account of early 'Bonn period'

    Bibliography

Fig. 1.1   An essay plan.

research', bearing in mind that not all the stages outlined there will be relevant to shorter writing projects.

4 Drafting

You may go through several drafts before you feel ready to write up the final version; don't assume that one draft will be enough. If your ideas are very clear, you plan very well, and the piece you are writing is short, then you may only need one draft, but it is much more common to need more. (On the other hand, of course, you have to learn when to stop. You cannot go on drafting and redrafting indefinitely. Your goal should be simply to construct a sound argument that fulfils the requirements of the question or title, not to write the perfect essay, or thesis, or book. There is no such thing.)

As you write your draft (or drafts), you should refer back frequently to both the essay title and your plan, to check that you are answering the question. As I said earlier, you may feel that your original plan needs some reworking at this stage. The following points should help you to learn how to put together a sound and relevant argument.

The basic structure of an essay should take the following form:

- an introduction;
- the main body;
- a conclusion.

The introduction and conclusion should each take up a single paragraph, while the main body of the essay will require a number of paragraphs. The following points should be included.

INTRODUCTION

- Your introduction should address the keywords of the title.
- You should show your awareness of the most important problems, ideas or debates suggested by those keywords, and indicate how you are going to approach these issues yourself.

For example, in Fig. 1.1 the essay title has suggested three points to the writer: the first two are the main points that the writer has learnt about the periodization of Beethoven's work; the third indicates that the writer intends to examine the three-period idea with some caution. (The writer has been careful to establish *only* those problems, ideas and debates relevant to *this particular essay title*, and has not fallen into the trap of addressing 'Beethoven's creative output' in more general terms.)

THE MAIN BODY

- It is important to be clear about your conclusion, because the main body of your essay should build towards it.
- You should organize the main points of your argument into a logical series of connected paragraphs. (As a rule of thumb, devote one paragraph to discussion of each main point.)
- You should check that each paragraph of your essay is a stepping stone taking the reader one stage closer to the conclusion. Paragraphing should help the reader to follow the argument.

For example, in Fig. 1.1 the most obvious and appropriate way to structure the essay is by dealing with each of the three periods in turn. But if the writer were to try to fit everything about each period into one paragraph, there would be three over-sized paragraphs, which would not be helpful to the reader. Rather, Fig. 1.1 implies the subdivision of each period into several paragraphs. Defining the period may or may not provide enough material to form a paragraph in its own right. If not, it could fit with discussion of the characteristics of the period to form one paragraph. Discussing an illustration of Beethoven's work from the period will probably form another paragraph, and presenting the objections or anomalies another.

CONCLUSION

- A conclusion should never introduce completely new material or ideas that you have not discussed in the essay.
- It should give a direct response to the question or issue raised in the essay title. Whether you answer 'yes' or 'no', or give a more cautious 'on the one hand…, but on the other hand…' response, you should make your judgement clear.
- If you have argued the main part of the essay clearly and logically, there should be no need for an elaborate, lengthy or complex conclusion. Indeed, a conclusion benefits from being clear, succinct and straightforward. You should not repeat the entire argument; rather, you should give a simple answer backed up by a brief summary (in a few sentences) of the main evidence that supports it.

For example, in Fig. 1.1 the writer concludes simply that there are some merits to the three-period idea, but that there are indeed reasons to treat it with caution. However, before stating this, the writer intends to summarize what the merits and the problems are. This is important – it supports the final concluding point and gives it authority and substance.

5 Checking your work (editing and proof-reading)

Checking what you have written is a crucial part of the process of writing, and it is not a simple question of reading your work through quickly. Two fundamental stages are involved – editing and proof-reading – and they are quite separate, though obviously closely related. You cannot cover both adequately at the same time: they require two separate re-readings.

When you *edit* your work, you are thinking primarily of the content. You need to consider whether you have fulfilled your task, and whether your style is appropriate to that task. You need also to think about areas such as grammar, structure and factual accuracy. In other words, you are concerned at this stage with the accuracy and comprehensibility of your argument. The editing stage should take place *before* you write up the final version.

Proof-reading is the final checking stage, and if you have done your editing carefully it should not give rise to too many corrections. When you proof-read, you should think primarily of matters of detail. This means checking for spelling and typing errors, and making a last check for consistency in areas such as the bibliography and the numbering of illustrations. It also means re-covering a lot of ground that you have already covered in the editing stage, but this time you should be confident that you no longer need to check the bigger issues such as the coherence of your argument or factual accuracy.

When you submit your essay, it should contain the following elements:

- a title (and your name, unless, for example, your examination board requires the work to be anonymous);
- an explanation of terms and abbreviations, if necessary (prior explanations are useful for clarifying special terminologies or abbreviations you have used);

- the essay itself;
- the bibliography (see Chapter 4);
- an appendix containing music extracts and pictures, if necessary (see Chapter 5).

Writing in examinations

Examinations are always something of a worry, but many candidates make them more difficult than they need be by not preparing properly, by not having an examination technique and by not practising that technique. The formats for examinations and musical tests vary considerably. The secret of preparing for examinations is to concentrate on understanding what you are to be examined on, rather than slavishly trying to memorize facts. The 'facts' will be easier to remember if you understand their importance. The advice here is restricted to some general points that might help your approach to a written examination.

- Make sure you know the format of the examination paper a considerable time before the examination itself.
- Look at previous relevant examination papers to work out the types of questions set and the content they cover.
- Use these previous examination papers (or invent questions of your own) and practise writing under examination conditions (that is, within a time limit and without the use of reference material).
- In the examination, spend about 10% of the time reading the questions and understanding them. Do not try to rationalize the question to fit the question you hoped and revised for.
- Spend about 20% of your time planning your answers in note form. This might seem like a long time, but it will be time well spent as it will make the writing of your answers faster and more efficient. Plan by jotting down the meaning of the question and the points you will make in your answer. Order your points in a logical progression.
- Spend about 60% of the time writing. Write short clear sentences, never try to write too much – quality is more important than quantity – and, above all, address the question. Try to give concrete examples that support what you are saying. Don't attempt to fit in irrelevant facts merely because you remember them.

- Spend the remaining 10% of the time checking what you have written. Concentrate on checking for obvious errors and places where your meaning may not appear clear.
- Answer all the sections of the paper that are required. You award yourself a zero grade for every required part of the paper you do not answer. Even if you feel you know little about the topic, address the question logically, use your wider knowledge to make intelligent guesses, and write something down. This may get you more marks than you imagine.

Writing CD liner notes

CD liner notes (and programme notes) vary enormously. There is no single format for them. But, as is the case with programme notes, liner notes have become something of a genre. While there is no set rule for the way they should be laid out, the notes themselves should be interesting and accessible. The works referred to must be placed in some sort of context, and enough information about them must be provided for readers to find out more if they want to – even if they do so just by looking at a music dictionary. Clearly the information you give must be accurate. Obtain scores of the works that are performed, and also do some research (see Chapters 2, 3 and 8) in order to make your text authoritative. The following formal elements should be included. They can be distributed in appropriate sections of the notes:

- The title of each piece, its context if it is extracted from a larger work and the catalogue or opus number if it has one. (The way that this and other relevant information is properly written is explained in Chapter 7.)
- The duration of each track.
- The commonly used name of the composer and his or her dates. If the composer is still alive you should give the birth date (b. 1945).
- The name of the author of any words that are set (and the name of the translator if there is one).
- The name of the arrangers if there are any (see Chapter 7).
- If it is possible and practicable, the full text of vocal music should be given in the language in which it is being sung. If this is not English, a translation should also be given.

- The names of performers should be given in the form that is preferred by them. The names of soloists, accompanists and conductor should certainly be given. It is also usual to give the names of chamber music performers and members of bands. It is less usual to give the names of members of symphony orchestras or large choruses.
- Where soloists or otherwise well-known individuals or small groups are involved, short biographical notes on the performers may be provided.
- The instruments that performers play should be given in their full rather than abbreviated form (see pages 132–3). However, standard abbreviations can be used if, for example, players play more than one instrument and these need to be identified on individual tracks.
- In period-instrument performances with historic or historical instruments (see pages 131 and 137), the makers of the instruments that are used should be identified. Any other interesting information relevant to such matters (such as the pitch or temperament that is used in the performance) might also be noted.

While it is not usually necessary to use the formal citation conventions described in Chapter 4 in non-scholarly publications such as CD liner or programme notes, it is nevertheless helpful to give readers sufficient information to enable them to find interesting information that you mention in your writing. This can usually be done effectively by giving key details – the name of the author, the title of the book and the date of its publication – in the flow of your text:

> Peter Barrow, in his 1981 book *Second-hand Music*, was the first to draw attention to the extent to which this work uses themes borrowed from Mozart.

However, when you quote a substantial passage from a printed work it may be worth giving not only the author, title and date, but also the relevant page number(s).

Writing concert programme notes

Writing programme notes is a task that confronts most musicians at some time or other. Increasingly the authorship of programme notes figures in the assessment in music courses and examination syllabuses.

The important thing to remember about concert programme notes is
that they have three key functions:
- to give details of the works and performers;
- to give contextual information about the programme and each
  work in it that will help the audience understand the music
  (remember that programme notes are usually read through, not
  studied);
- to give enough detail for the audience to be able to find out more
  about a piece – this means that the details of each work must be
  full and accurate.

Much of the information given above for CD liner notes is also relevant for programme notes. However, there are differences between
CD and programme notes:
- The names of all performers and their instruments/voices (including orchestra and choir members) should normally be given.
- In some concerts – especially period-instrument performances –
  individual players perform on several different instruments. To
  acknowledge each instrument that each player uses for every item
  could make the programme seem cluttered. Whether or not this
  is done depends on the case in question, but a good compromise
  is to identify all the instruments a performer plays against the
  name of that performer, and just identify the instruments used
  for individual items.
- Some programme notes (for operas, for example) are glossy and
  extensive, with librettos and essays about the composer, the plot
  and the production. But much shorter programme notes can be
  effective too. There is considerable flexibility about what you say
  and how the notes are arranged, but remember that the audience
  has to read the notes relatively quickly, and that they are intended
  to help them enjoy the concert. Here are some elements to think
  about:
  i) Say something about the context of each piece in terms of the
     composer's output – whether it is a late or an early piece, why
     it was written and so on. Was it revised by the original
     composer or by another composer? If so, which version is
     being performed?
  ii) Do you have information about the reception of the first
     performance?

iii) Is there anything that the audience should know about the way the piece is going to be performed? Are period instruments being used? Are movements being left out? Do not give a detailed analysis of works (unless you really have to) and avoid using music notation unless there are reasons why it would be appropriate to do so. You have to make a decision about the level of technical complexity that you introduce into programme notes. It is usually more important to signal significant points that the audience might listen out for than to give a detailed formal analysis. Not all audience members are the same: some are regular concert-goers with a good knowledge of music, others will be less knowledgeable. Striking the right balance is difficult but important. It is usually perfectly possible to make interesting and even challenging points about music without resorting to technical language.

iv) Do some research into each piece. If you come across something that is really interesting and illuminating, you will probably find that your audience will be similarly interested by it.

Writing reviews

Reviews are among the most important and widely-read forms of writing about music. They are a powerful means through which musicians and the public in general keep in touch with the latest information about performances, publications and recordings. They contribute to thinking and discourse about music in innumerable ways. Here, as with other forms of writing, there are a variety of different approaches. Professional reviewers – those who write for national newspapers and magazines, for example – often reveal a remarkable gift for providing highly readable, erudite information and critique in very few words. On the other hand, review articles in academic journals, such as the *Journal of the Royal Musical Association*, are often extensive, and provide a detailed appraisal of books or recordings in the context of the area to which they contribute.

The type of publication in which a review is to appear will largely determine its format, tone and length. However, most good reviews, whether they are of concerts, publications or recordings, have three main elements:

- *Information about the subject of the review*. In the case of a performance this will include information about the performers, and the date and place of the performance, as well as information about the programme. There is no need to detail the entire content of the programme if many pieces are performed. Reviews of publications or recordings should begin by giving enough information for the reader to be able to obtain the publication or recording in question. This will include bibliographical or discographical information and the price. The citation formats given elsewhere in this book could be used, but popular publications often adopt a more relaxed approach. National daily newspapers can provide a good model for concert reviews, and magazines such as *Gramophone* have very clear formats for CD reviews.

- *Contextual comments*. The best reviews often address not simply the reviewed performance or publication in its own right, but also broader issues that may help the listener's or reader's understanding and inform their judgement. In the case of a performance, it is particularly appropriate to comment on the challenges and points of interest that are associated with the works. Some of the issues discussed in the section headed 'Some questions to ask when writing about musical works' (page 7) could be helpful in this respect. If the review is of a publication (a book or a music edition, for example), it is helpful to compare it to related publications.

- *The evaluation*. I have used the word 'evaluation' rather than 'criticism' because it is important to see the reviewer as a *mediator* between the performance or publication and people who may not have heard or read the subject of the review. Reviews should be fair and balanced. This does not mean that all reviews should say something good and something bad: some performances and publications are so good that an excellent review is appropriate, while others are irredeemably diabolical. But it is never appropriate to condemn or praise a performance or publication without giving good reasons. The best reviews are those that convey a taste of the performance or publication, and contain the sense of an argument in their evaluation; they help the reader understand the subject of the review rather than merely convey prejudices.

Writing for reading aloud

This is a special topic. It is common for musicians to have to give talks, lectures and other types of public speeches. Off-the-cuff speeches are fine, but the delivery of academic papers and special lectures or presentations requires a more systematic approach. Even experienced music academics and performers *read* lectures if they have important and detailed information to convey. Here are some hints:

- Find out how long you are expected to speak for, and allow yourself a shorter time (by a few minutes) than you are given.
- Prepare your text in double spacing – it is easier to read.
- Time yourself reading one page of double-spaced typed text aloud – this will give you a guide for how many pages you can write to fill your allotted time.
- Do not try to mimic a conversational style when you write. Write what you mean to say, and adjust the style later if you think that the language needs to be softened. But do not do this if it means obscuring the meaning of what you want to convey.
- Give thought to the type of audience you will be addressing and try to estimate how much they will know about your subject. Striking the right level is difficult. Remember that your audience will hear your words only once: they will not be able to re-read a sentence or two as they could if it were a written paper.
- Use visual and aural illustrations if you can, but remember that these will take up some of your allotted time.
- Above all, rehearse. Read your paper aloud several times; even play and/or show your illustrations. Mark pauses, phrases and emphases on your script just as if it were a piece of music. This type of preparation is really important, particularly if you are not experienced.

Bibliography

Chambers, E., and A. Northedge, *The Arts Good Study Guide* (Milton Keynes: The Open University, 1997).

Creme, P., and M. Lea, *Writing at University: A Guide for Students* (Buckingham: Open University Press, 1997).

Dunleavy, P., *Studying for a Degree in the Humanities and Social Sciences* (London: Macmillan Education, 1986).

Seely, J., *The Oxford Guide to Writing and Speaking* (Oxford University Press, 1998).

Chapter two

DOING RESEARCH: A BASIC METHOD FOR LONGER PROJECTS

'DOING RESEARCH' can mean simply looking for information in a relaxed and casual way. But if it is important for you to obtain accurate, authoritative and relevant information without wasting time, you need to have a method. All researchers develop a method that suits them best. This chapter provides suggestions for the basis of a systematic research method.

Writing up and presenting the results of research requires special skills too, so this chapter also deals with the way that research can be written up and presented. Sometimes you undertake research so that you can describe and explain something accurately. Description has its place in writings about music, and this type of writing probably constitutes most of what the majority of people read about music; programme notes, newspaper articles and many of the writings that are the basis of radio broadcasts fall into this category. But in some writings, especially in academic work and informed criticism, research has a more substantial purpose: you undertake research in order to understand your subject better and to acquire evidence which can then form the basis of a written argument. Much of what I have to say in this chapter is aimed at research that is intended to lead to a longer piece of academic writing, in particular an undergraduate or postgraduate dissertation or thesis, or a diploma submission. However, anyone with less demanding objectives should find the processes I describe helpful, because any level of investigation is likely to be more effective if it is well organized and systematic.

A note on sources – primary and secondary

Throughout this and other chapters of this book I use the word 'sources'. It is important to understand what it means in terms of research. It is also important to be able to distinguish between the two main types of source that researchers encounter: primary and secondary. This topic could fill a book in its own right; all I wish to do here is to introduce you to the terms so that you can investigate them more thoroughly and gain a better understanding of them.

A source is evidence of any type that you use when conducting research. It can be a printed or handwritten document; it can be published or unpublished. But sources are not restricted to written words. Written or recorded music, paintings, photographs, musical instruments, interviews with composers or performers, plans of concert halls, video recordings, newspaper articles and advertisements all constitute sources for research. In fact, there can be no defined limit on what counts as a source for research.

Any type of source can have special importance in a research project, but scholars make a distinction between:

- *primary sources:* the raw materials that are being researched;
- *secondary sources:* those that are not raw materials, but which nevertheless interpret or inform our understanding of the raw materials.

So, for example, primary sources for a Chopin étude would include the original published edition of the étude in question, as well as original manuscripts. Secondary sources would include modern articles about the Chopin études.

The characteristics of good research projects

There are many types of research project. They have different objectives, and particular methodologies are appropriate to these objectives. Some projects result in a musical performance or a presentation in some other medium. But my aim is to offer advice that will help you produce a good piece of *written* work. It could be called a thesis, essay, dissertation, chapter, article or whatever.

It is worth keeping in mind that most really successful written work demonstrates the following characteristics:

- It is clearly written so that everyone who reads it gets from it the meaning that the writer intends to convey.
- It is suited to its purpose.

In addition, it demonstrates some or all of the following:

- It is well presented and uses the necessary scholarly conventions consistently and correctly.
- It is interesting, authoritative and free of factual errors.
- It uses illustrations, descriptions and quotations accurately and with proper acknowledgements.
- It goes beyond mere description and demonstrates that the investigation has been probing, and that the evidence gathered establishes arguments and conclusions. This is one of the defining characteristics of good academic writing.
- There is a logical relationship between the conclusions and the evidence that has been used in order to reach them.

There is not a single, simple formula for conducting research, because, as I have said, different topics may demand different approaches, but research is conducted more easily and efficiently if you adopt a systematic approach. This systematic approach applies to the way a project is designed, conducted and presented.

Structuring research

A research project can be thought of as having five stages. Most of this chapter is devoted to my explanation and illustration of how this five-stage approach can make a research project rewarding and successful. It is not the only method that can be adopted, but this is one that works.

- *Design stage.* At this stage you need to think broadly about what it is that you want and feel able to investigate. You need to read about your subject, and, if you have chosen your own topic, ask yourself searching questions to test whether it is the right thing for you to be doing. Some projects (such as high-school disserta-tions) are set for you. In these cases you need to think carefully about the task that has been set for you and what it requires of you (see Chapter 1).
- *Initial research stage.* This is the stage (which you will have dipped into in the design stage) where you take stock of the reading that you need to do, and become acquainted with the main writings of others who have worked on your topic. At this stage you are still spending part of your time planning your way forward.
- *Detailed research stage.* At this point you focus on what you have

determined to be the key area that you need to investigate. For less demanding tasks you may not need to go further than reading two or three key published texts, but for postgraduate work this will almost certainly mean that you will be looking at important primary sources: manuscripts, newspapers, publications or scores from the period related to the theme you are investigating.

• *Synthesis stage.* Here you need to consider the raw information that you have obtained: how it can be used to form an argument or exposition of your subject, and whether it can be corroborated, refined or abandoned. To an extent, you are synthesizing inform-ation at every stage, but there comes a point when you have to stop finding things out and consider the evidence you have accumulated. This is much easier to deal with if you have a really clear method for storing information as you find it. It is yet easier if you have a system for recognizing the relationship between different pieces of evidence as you are researching.

• *Presentation stage.* This is the final phase, where you write up your expositions and arguments, and arrange your material so that it is clearly presented and contains the emphasis you wish it to have.

In the sections that follow I explain these five stages in more detail, but I should reiterate that this approach can be the *basis* for a system-atic research method. You should amend it to suit your needs and circumstances. It is not my intention to imply that research is entirely mechanistic.

1 Designing a research project

If you are in a position to choose the topic for your project, whether it be a school project, a PhD thesis or something yet more ambitious, you should give thought to some practicalities. You should take time when devising a research project, read about it and see whether the topic really sparks your interest or whether your enthusiasm for it wanes easily. The following could act as a checklist at this stage. But it is not a checklist merely to be glanced at: it is to be considered seriously and worked at. You must put yourself under scrutiny. Ask yourself searching questions about your proposed topic and do not settle on it until you have provided yourself with convincing answers to the following:

- Does the topic *really* interest you, and is it likely to sustain your interest over the duration of the project? This is one of the most important questions of all. The best research topic for you is one that is likely to keep firing your curiosity even when you have setbacks or are engaged in some of the more boring tasks that have to be undertaken in any research project.

- Does it build on your strengths and avoid major calls on your weaknesses? For example, avoid topics that might require you to spend time looking at texts in foreign languages if you have no competence in those languages. If you are interested in performance and repertoire, or in the history of an instrument, choose a topic that your own experience as a musician might shed light on. A good idea is to list the types of activity that a research topic might require: reading academic writings, studying manuscripts, editing music, studying musical scores, reading old newspapers, listening to archive recordings, conducting interviews, looking at topics that draw on other subjects – social or economic history, philosophy and popular culture, for example. How do these activities rate in terms of your interests and competencies? The essential question to ask yourself is whether you are well prepared to conduct this research, or whether you would have to learn new skills – other than research techniques – in order to do it. You need not turn your back on an idea because it will involve learning new skills, but you must assess what you need to do, and be realistic about what it will take (in terms of time, for example) to do it.

- Does your project serve its purpose well? For example, does it meet the demands specified by your school or university? PhD students are required to complete projects that make an original contribution to knowledge. If you are in this position you should be sure that your topic has this potential. Test how many people have worked on topics similar to yours – you will find advice on how to do this in the books listed at the end of this chapter and in Chapter 8 below. It is important for me to emphasize that no book (including this one) can usurp the function of the regulations of an academic examining body. If you conduct research in candidature for an examination, you must have a clear understanding of what you are required to do and you must meet those requirements. But equally it is reasonable to expect any organization that has accepted your candidature to provide you with clear advice on what is expected of you, and to inform you of what you have to do in order to do well. If these things are not clear to you, you should take steps to clarify them.

- Is it practicable for you to conduct this project? Are there any barriers that you might encounter when trying to investigate material that is vital for it? What are the main sources (books, manuscripts or other items) that you would examine as the core work for your research? Are they conveniently situated for you, or would you have to travel long distances in order to examine them? Is there any other restriction on access to your sources? Sometimes research projects are chosen because the researcher has easy access to a body of sources – such as a specialist library or archive – that suggests a ready-made topic for investigation. There is nothing wrong with basing your project on sources that are easily available to you.

- How are you going to limit the breadth of the subject that you will investigate? Badly designed research topics imply an almost limitless field of study. You must choose a theme and period for your study that helps you control the way you will investigate it. Most projects are limited by one or more of the following factors: a defined topic or theme; a period; and some other feature such as a geographical area. For instance, a project title such as 'Musical education in Melbourne between *c.*1850 and *c.*1895' illustrates all three factors.

- Is your topic too limiting and restrictive? Although a good research topic is one that is well planned, the very process of conducting research – even well-planned research – can lead to a revelation that will cause you to make an adjustment to your original topic idea. You should therefore plan your investigation in a way that accommodates some flexibility. Most examination regulations (especially undergraduate and postgraduate regulations) acknowledge that such flexibility is not just necessary but desirable.

2 Initial research

Some of the initial research on a topic is done when you are designing it. But once you have decided on the topic, you need to review the work that has been done by others on the subject. This is best done by identifying one or two books or articles that seem to be key texts for the subject. At this stage you would be reading widely in the area suggested by your subject topic. For example, if you were interested in the music of Tommy Dorsey (1905–56), you would be looking not just for texts about Dorsey, but also about American jazz during the period when he was most active. You may then find that the works of certain writers about Dorsey seem to be particularly valued and respected. A good way of organizing your initial reading is to move systematically from the broader picture to your specific topic. Background reading for a topic concerning the music of Tommy Dorsey might be organized in a series of stages:

i)   books about the history of the USA in the period when Dorsey was alive;

ii) books about the history of jazz in general;

iii) publications about jazz at the time Dorsey was playing;

iv) publications about Dorsey's life and work.

One of the most important places to look for sources is in the bibliographies of specialist books. (Bibliographies are discussed in Chapter 4.) Of course, no book will provide bibliographical details of books and articles that were completed after that book was published. But this is a good starting point. For more recent publications you would need to search in library catalogues and Internet sites using subject keywords. The means by which you do this are described in Chapter 3.

The initial research phase of your project has a number of important objectives. You should be acutely aware of these and again pose yourself questions to test whether you are achieving them. If this phase of your work is going well, you should be gaining a sense of expertise. You should feel that:

• It has made you broadly aware of basic facts concerning your project: for example (if relevant), the dates, biography and output of a composer or performer, or the primary technical developments of a musical instrument and why certain works for that instrument acquired a high status.

- It has given you a clear idea of the historical, sociological and musical context for your topic.
- It has given you a broad sense of the scholarship of your subject: who the most important authorities are, what their significant writings are and why they have gained respect. Often it is easy to discern that there is a group of periodicals that seem especially relevant to your subject.
- It has given you a clear idea of the body of evidence that seems to be the main focus for your subject. You should have gained a feeling of what the areas of controversy are: what issues are being debated, and whether those debates seem to revolve around a particular point of discussion.
- It has provided you with enough information and ideas to be able to construct a schedule for the remainder of your project. It should have enabled you to define firstly the material to which you should give more careful scrutiny (this may include returning to some of the materials that you have looked at already), and secondly the material that will form the essential body of evidence for your investigation.
- You have established a sound, reliable methodology for doing research, and have designed a good, clear and accurate method for storing information and the ideas that you glean from that information.

Storing research data

The way you store research information or data (hence the use of the term 'database' to describe such a store) is one of the most important features of systematic research. If you do not design a good system for doing this, you will waste time, run the risk of being inaccurate and perhaps limit your ability to look at evidence in a way that reveals vital thematic relationships and tendencies.

Remember that days, weeks or even years after you have scrutinized a book or some other research source, your notes will be the only record of the information you have found. It is vital that you keep information in a way that will be as comprehensible to you then as it was when you wrote it down. In short, the database you establish should enable you to:

- store information succinctly;

- record (exactly) where that information comes from;
- find relevant information easily;
- help you recognize that some pieces of data share certain features or have special relevance to one of the themes of your research.

Most research databases are now kept on computer, and several of the special programmes for databases are impressively powerful and versatile. But any computer programme, irrespective of its versatility and power, is worthless if the data that is fed into it is unsophisticated, badly selected or inaccurate. In this book I cannot provide advice on how to deal with specific computer databases, because each programme operates somewhat differently. But it is possible to illustrate how they work by explaining the main features that are common to systems for data storage. In fact, the example I give here can be used to organize data even if you do not have a computer, by using the more old-fashioned method of storing information on index cards. This is a perfectly satisfactory way of learning how to organize and use a simple database.

The system I suggest is one that uses three separate but related sets of records, each one storing different types, but related fields, of information:

a) *Bibliographical records* in which you record the details of each source that you have used. These records are stored in alphabetical order.

b) *Data records* that record the notes and quotations you make when studying each source. These records are kept in numerical order: each is given a number, and you store them in the order in which you make them.

c) *Keyword records* that are intended to help you find the information you have stored in the bibliographical and data records. You create keywords that suit your needs ('instruments', 'voices', 'composers', for example), and note under each heading where you have stored the relevant information. These records are stored in alphabetical order.

The three sets of records (in a computer database they would be called information 'fields') are described below in a little more detail and with illustrations. Remember that this is intended as the basis for a system that suits you. You may want to adjust it or make it more elaborate to suit your purpose.

BIBLIOGRAPHICAL RECORDS *(see Fig. 2.1)*

It is possible for all types of sources to be stored in a single alphabetical sequence, but it is usually better to have one index for published works, another for manuscripts and musical works, and others for visual representations, sound recordings and so on. When you consult a source (read a book, listen to a recording or whatever), the first thing you must do is to write a bibliographical/discographical reference for it by:

- using one of the formal citation conventions described in Chapters 4 and 9–11;
- giving each record a unique abbreviated reference. For published works you can use either the author–date method or the short-title method (see Chapters 4 and 9). For manuscripts use the library sigla (see Chapter 11). For other media you can use an appropriate device – these too are listed in Chapters 10 and 11. All these methods allow you to store data in alphabetical or numerical order.

You should be consistent in this, because if you do not keep to a particular system, you will waste vast amounts of time when you are writing up your project. It is essential that the bibliographical system you use for these records is the one that you will use in your final presentation, otherwise you will have to reformat the entire bibliography at a later date. This is especially important if you use a computer database programme, because such programmes make the final preparation of a bibliography (which can be extremely time-consuming) easy and efficient.

DATA RECORDS *(see Fig. 2.2)*

These contain the notes you write when you are researching: quotations, references to important parts of a text that are too long to quote, your opinion of a piece of writing, your paraphrases and summary of a text, and so on. It is crucial that you distinguish between the quotation of a text and your paraphrase of it by using quotation marks, square brackets and ellipses correctly. (These devices are described in Chapter 6.)

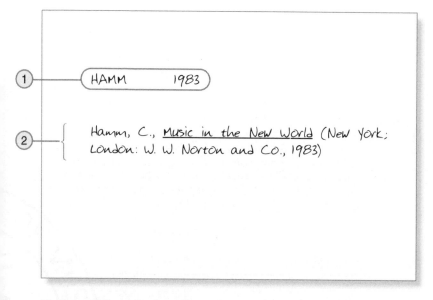

Fig. 2.1 **Bibliographical record**

These cards are stored in alphabetical order and contain full citation information about each source that has been consulted.

① Name of the author (and date of the publication) – signalling the place in the alphabetical sequence in which it is filed.

② Full citation.

Additionally you should:

- identify the data-record number in the top left-hand corner;
- identify the source that the notes are taken from at the top of the record on the right, using an abbreviation that matches the heading in the bibliographical index;
- identify the relevant page numbers at each point in your note-taking;
- identify in round brackets at the bottom of the record the theme or topic to which this record is relevant. I explain below why this is important.

KEYWORD RECORDS *(see Figs 2.3(a) and (b))*

Your personal database should be designed to accommodate any special features or subtleties that *you* want it to include. This part of the system is therefore personal and subjective: it should suit your

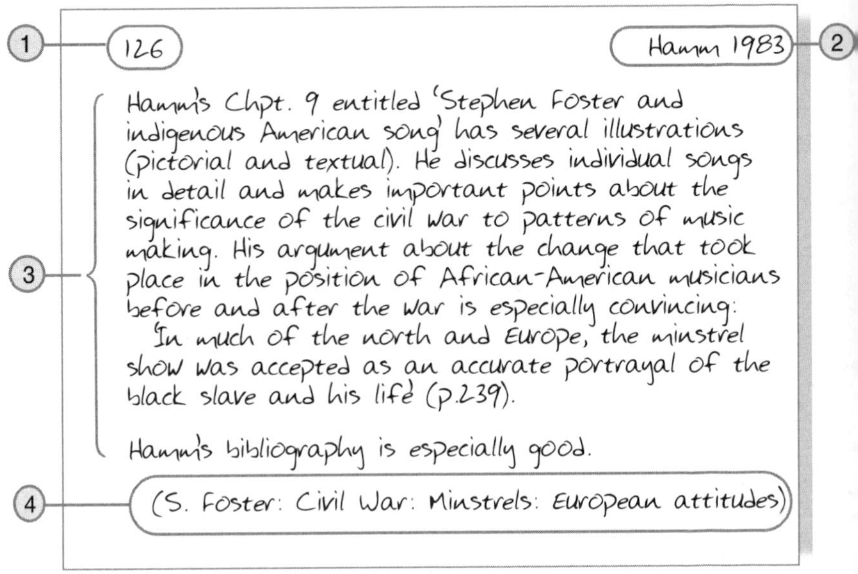

Fig. 2.2   **Data record**
Data cards contain notes that are made when consulting a source – they may be
continued on to more than one card if there is a lot of information. They are kept
in numerical order – cards are numbered and added to the collection in the order
you make them.
① Number of the card.
② The 'source' – this cross-references to the bibliography records.
③ The data. Brief notes including (if necessary) quotations. It is important to
   make a note of page numbers; you may need to refer to them in footnotes.
④ A summary of the keywords to which this source might be relevant.

vision of how you want to investigate your topic. The keyword
records have headings that relate to themes in your research. For
example, if you were working on a subject such as 'Music in New
Zealand in the 1920s', I can imagine that the following themes or
keywords might be appropriate: 'Orchestras', 'Music teachers',
'Reception' (meaning the way that audiences and critics respond to
music), 'Repertoire', 'Church music', 'Composers', 'Light music',
'Jazz', 'Personalities', 'Instruments' – the list could go on. The records
under each of these themes would contain references to the unique
numbers of relevant data records and also to key texts that might cast
particular light on these themes.

(a)

(b)

Fig. 2.3(a) and Fig. 2.3(b)   **Keyword records**

In Fig. 2.3(a) the keyword card shows which of the 'data records' contain information about minstrels. In Fig. 2.3(b) it shows which of them contain information about the composer Stephen Foster.

① Keyword.

② References to data records (sometimes with annotations).

3 Detailed research

It is essential that you record information meticulously, and you should take notes even if you are simply recording what is sometimes called 'negative data' – you should note that a particular source holds no relevant information (otherwise, you could end up looking at the same source twice).

Throughout this stage of your work you should be trying to gain two perspectives simultaneously:

- an understanding of the detail that your scrutiny of individual sources is revealing;
- a view of the way that such detail informs the wider picture or argument that is emerging from your investigation.

In addition, you should (if you are doing postgraduate research) keep looking at publishers' catalogues and journal abstracts, to see whether new information has been published that is relevant to your work.

One of the dangers at this stage is that you can become obsessive about detail at the expense of the broader picture. This can affect the efficiency of your research. One of the pitfalls is to assume that most answers can be found in sources unique to or emanating from the world of music. A great deal of music research is informed and enriched by different subjects. Music should be seen in a wider artistic, social and even economic context. If you encounter a problem in obtaining information, you should ask yourself whether it is likely that you are the first person to have needed this information. The answer is almost certainly that you are not, and that someone has not only found the information you are looking for but has written about it. Take, for example, a topic that involves the history of a particular musical instrument. Among the most important sources for such a study are pictures and other visual representations of instruments. The place to find information about such images may not be in books about musical instruments, but in the work of art historians who may have not only catalogued the subjects of different pictures but made detailed studies of the subjects and contexts revealed in them. Some general resources are mentioned in Chapter 8.

4 Synthesis

This is the most difficult part to offer advice on, because research projects can cover so many different topics. I can only offer general guidance, based on problems commonly encountered by researchers:

- One of the most difficult things is to know when to stop researching and start writing. Even though my five 'stages' imply a chronological sequence – one stage follows on from the other when the former is completed – you should practise writing continuous text (as opposed to note-taking) *throughout the project*. But a point is eventually reached when you have stopped researching and you are faced with the task of writing up the result of your investigations.
- By this stage the final structure of what you are writing – chapters, sections or sub-headings – should suggest itself clearly. Create a structure and jot down the topics that you intend to deal with in each section or chapter of your work.
- Your research will already have led you to some conclusions about your topic. You should write down each conclusion and jot down the evidence for that conclusion.
- If you are allowed to do so, be prepared to refine your title a little. It is often best to amend a title rather than to force your ideas into one that no longer applies.
- Do not feel that all parts of your work need to be analytical: sections of it (such as the introduction and other prefatory material, and perhaps appendices) can be descriptive.
- You must be prepared to leave out a substantial proportion of the data you have accumulated. Do not be tempted to include information merely because it is interesting and attractive. To do so could distort your arguments and lead to a lack of clarity, relevance and focus.
- Be prepared to write at least two drafts. If you can get someone to read these for you and give you an appraisal of them, do so.

5 Presentation

Most longer forms of writing (such as dissertations) have the elements listed below. Each element starts on a new page:

- a title page giving the full title and (usually) the name of the author;
- a contents list giving the page numbers for each section;

- an abstract (a brief 300-word summary of what the work is about);
- acknowledgements (to people who have helped with your research and also those who have given permission for you to quote or reproduce illustrative material);
- explanation of terms and abbreviations (prior explanations are useful for clarifying special terminologies or abbreviations you have used);
- the chapters (each chapter has a number, and there are often sub-headings within chapters);
- an appendix or appendices (appendices normally contain tables or illustrations that are too substantial to put in the main text, and should be numbered Appendix 1, Appendix 2 and so on);
- bibliography (and discography, if there is one);
- index (this is not always necessary in academic dissertations).

As I explained in Chapter 1, it is essential that you check your work thoroughly. The following rules apply to any piece of academic writing, irrespective of how short or long it is:

- It must be free of factual and typographical errors.
- It must be clear – what you write should suggest only one meaning to your readers.
- Whatever citation style and other conventions you adopt, they must be used consistently.
- If you offer prior explanations of terms and abbreviations, make sure that you use them consistently. Do not invent abbreviations or conventions if you can use an existing model.
- Make sure that your presentation is typographically clear, neat and consistent. Consistency matters in this respect, as it does in others. The visual appearance of your work is important.

Bibliography

Phillips, E. M., and D. S. Pugh, *How to get a Ph.D.*, 2nd edn (Buckingham: Open University Press, 1994).

Seely, J., *The Oxford Guide to Writing and Speaking* (Oxford University Press, 1998).

Doctoral dissertations in music:
<http://www.music.indiana.edu/ddm/>

Archive of abstracts of dissertations in music:
<http://www.sun.rhbnc.ac.uk/Music/Links/index.html>

(See also Chapter 8.)

Chapter three

USING LIBRARIES AND THE INTERNET

Using libraries

There are various types of libraries. The best collections of books and other media that provide information on music will be found in specialist institutions such as universities, and many universities allow the general public to have access to their collections for reference purposes. There are also many excellent music reference collections in public libraries. Increasingly public libraries provide not only books and recorded sound, but also Internet access. There are a number of directories of libraries that you can consult to help you locate the specialist libraries that will be of most use to you (see the bibliography at the end of this chapter for relevant books and Web sites). Check with your nearest large public library or university library whether it keeps these publications, either as printed copies or as CD-ROMs or on-line (electronic) databases. But bear in mind that you will almost certainly need to be a member of a library before it will let you use on-line resources other than its own catalogue.

If you wish to use a particular library, and especially if it is some distance from your home, it is a good idea to contact the library before you go to the trouble of visiting it, in order to check:

- whether you need to join before you can be admitted;
- whether there is a fee for joining;
- what membership allows you to do – for instance, whether you will be allowed to borrow books or simply use them on the premises for reference;
- whether you need such things as a passport photo (for your reader's ticket or pass) or the signature of a tutor or someone else in a position of authority who can verify your need to use the library.

When you start to use a new library, allow yourself an initial visit, or at least a couple of extra hours, so that you can get used to the layout of the library and the way its systems work. For instance, in some *reference libraries* such as The British Library (that is, libraries where you cannot borrow books) you must order the material you wish to look at, and wait while a librarian finds it and brings it to you. This means that you will need to find out how to place your order, how long you are likely to wait for it, and what you could be doing while you wait so as to make the most of your time. For instance, some general reference books are likely to be on the open shelves (that is, accessible to the reader without a librarian's assistance), so you could use the time to look things up in these, or to look for further references in the library catalogue. (It may be possible to order material by e-mail or telephone before you make your visit, but check how many days' notice and exactly how much information about the material the librarians will require in order to do this.)

It is also a good idea to familiarize yourself with the classification system used by the library (that is, the method by which the books are catalogued), and, if you will physically have to find the books and take them off the shelves, *where* in the library building the different classes are kept. For instance, many libraries use the Dewey Decimal Classification. This system divides areas of knowledge into ten classes, and then further subdivides them within those classes. The ten main classes are:

000   General works
100   Philosophy
200   Religion
300   Social sciences
400   Languages
500   Science
600   Technology
700   Arts and recreations
800   Literature
900   Geography, biography and history

700 is the class that includes music books, and the sub-classification for music is 780. Within that sub-classification, the different areas of music are further divided up as follows:

781   General principles and musical forms
782   Vocal music
783   Music for single voices. The voice

784   Instruments and instrumental ensembles
785   Ensembles with one instrument per part
786   Keyboard and other instruments
787   Stringed instruments (chordophones)
788   Wind instruments (aerophones)
789   [unnamed]

All books that deal primarily with musical topics will be shelved together and will be marked (usually at the bottom of their spines) with a classmark (a series of numbers or a combination of numbers and letters) in the 780s. It is also worth giving some thought to whether any other classes might contain books relevant to your line of study. For instance, if your project is on sixteenth-century Italian music, you will probably need to consult general books on sixteenth-century Italian *history*, and you might find useful material in books on Italian Renaissance *art*.

All major libraries now have computerized catalogues and these are available at terminals within the library building (university library catalogues are also available through the Internet). In the following section I deal with the techniques for searching electronic library catalogues. One of the fundamentals of doing research in a library is that you have to gain a clear and intimate knowledge of where things are kept and how the catalogue system is organized. Many people do not use libraries to their maximum advantage because they do not know how the catalogues work, how to find things and what to do to obtain the information they need. People are also sometimes reluctant to ask for information because they feel shy or think that they will expose themselves as being ignorant.

Most libraries provide floor plans and explanations of their collections and how to find what you are looking for. But it is worth remembering that among the most valuable resources of any library are the staff who work there. Librarians are not merely people who catalogue, stack, issue and check in books. They are highly trained information-services experts with a wide knowledge of the main reference materials for a range of subjects. You will not find it difficult to persuade a librarian to help you understand a library system or help you with more specialist queries. Don't be shy about asking, and don't pretend you have understood something if you are still uncertain about it – even about the most basic terminologies. A library will only be really useful to you if you know how to use it to its full potential. You will benefit from advice best if you explain the context of your investigation to the librarian. But do not expect librarians to do your research for you. They will tell you how the library works, but it is your job to conduct the research.

If your own library does not contain the works you want, you may be able to order books through an 'interlibrary loan' scheme, whereby your library will borrow what you need from another library. However, you need to find out whether this will be necessary well before you need to use the books in question, because it can take some time to borrow books this way.

Searching electronic library catalogues

While different library catalogues may look different from each other, the differences are generally cosmetic. Most will present you with a 'menu' of search options from which to choose (Fig. 3.1). Probably the first two options in the list will be to search for an author's name

Code
1   Quick AUTHOR/TITLE enquiry
2   TITLE enquiry
3   SUBJECT enquiry
4   NAME enquiry
5   Alphabetical list of AUTHORS
6   Alphabetical list of SUBJECTS
7   CLASSMARK enquiry
8   List of PERIODICALS
9   ISBN number enquiry (Books added since 1984 only)
/   Return to main menu
?   Help

Fig. 3.1   An example of the screen options given for a basic library catalogue search.

or the title of a book, and it may well be that a basic search under author name or title will yield the precise work you are looking for or a relatively small number of records amongst which you can easily find the one you want. Another common option is a 'keyword' or 'subject keyword' search. This kind of search enables you to put in a term that defines your topic ('Indian music', for example), and search for works that cover the topic but may not include the precise phrase in their title.

But what if your search yields a huge number of records that it will take you hours to work through? Or maybe you want to do a speculative search, to see, for example, what has been published in your subject area in the last five years. In these cases, you need to do a more specific kind of search – that is, you need to include more elements than simply the author's name or the book title or keyword.

Some catalogues try to narrow down the search by encouraging you to give as much information as possible in the first place. They present you with a series of boxes including author name, title, subject, publisher, date and so on (Fig. 3.2). You can fill in some or all of these boxes. Clearly, the more information you fill in, the more you will narrow down your search. However, do not fill in any information about which you are not certain. The computer can only work with the information you give it; so if you type in, say, a publication date of 1997, when in fact the book you are looking for was published in 1998, the result will be a message telling you that your item could not be found.

Other catalogues will allow you to do an 'advanced search'. The precise way this works will differ in different libraries (sometimes it is a type called a 'Boolean search'), but the principle is to allow you to specify a number of terms that you want to find, and eliminate other terms that are irrelevant (Fig. 3.3).

Sometimes you also have the option of using a 'wildcard'. A wildcard is a symbol that takes the place of a letter or group of letters. It is a way of broadening your search by allowing you to find references to a whole group of similar or related words. The symbols may differ from database to database, but an asterisk (*) is one that is commonly used. So, for example, typing in 'music*' would find not only all references to 'music', but also all references to words beginning with the letters 'm-u-s-i-c-', such as 'musical', 'musician', 'musicology' and so on.

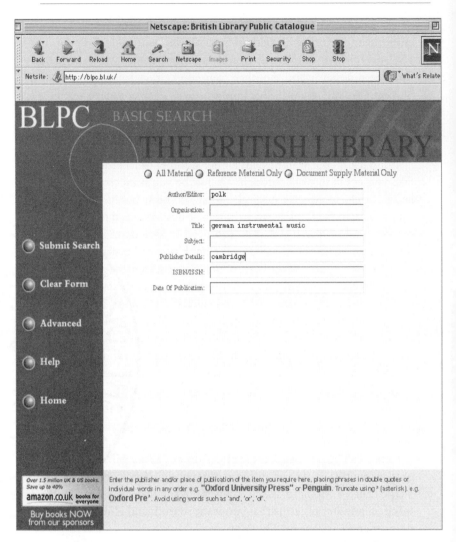

Fig. 3.2   A basic search screen (The British Library) with a wide set of options. The typing in the boxes will provide sufficient information to obtain full details of Keith Polk's book.

These advanced search techniques will also stand you in good stead for searching the World Wide Web, where you will find that most search engines give you the option of a basic search or a more refined one, and where a basic search will usually yield a vast number of results.

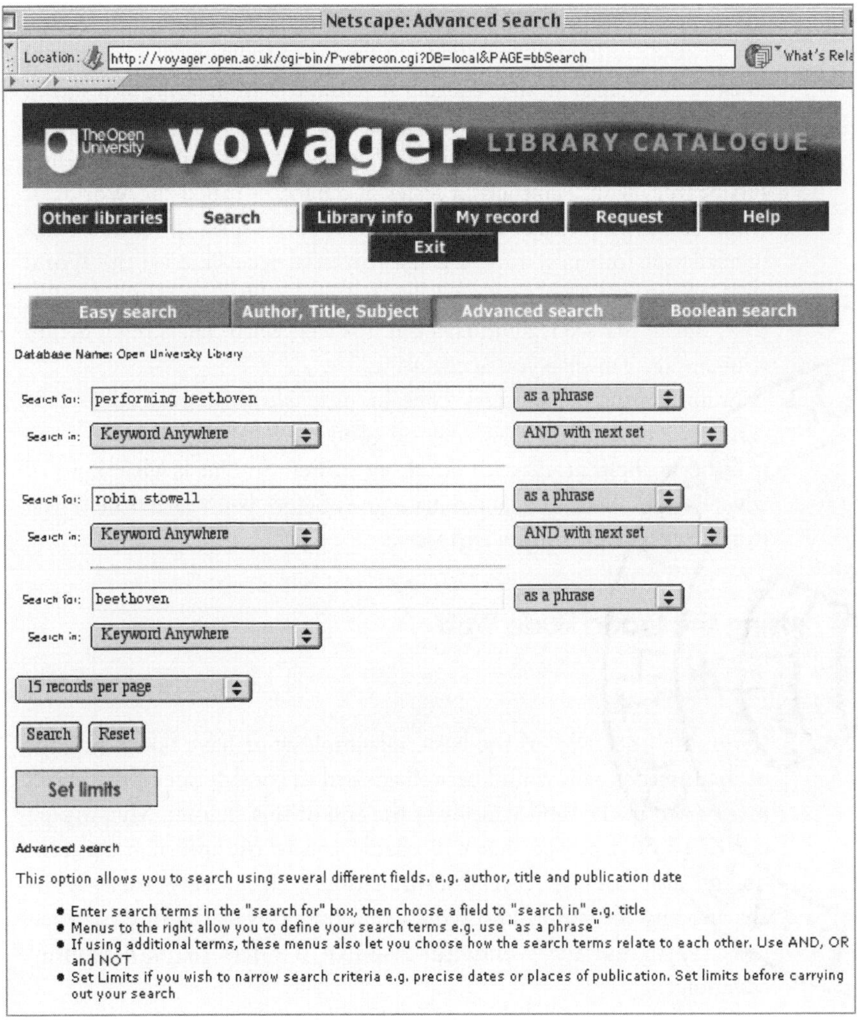

Fig. 3.3   An example of a yet more advanced search screen (The Open University).

In addition to the computerized catalogue of your own library, some huge bibliographical databases are available via the Internet. These do not enable you to *borrow* books (though some have a facility for purchasing them), but they do allow you to do extensive bibliographical searches and to check details about books. For example, the catalogues of The British Library and its American equivalent, the

Library of Congress, can be accessed via the Internet, as can university library catalogues worldwide. If you are a member of a university or other academic library, another invaluable bibliographical resource which you may be able to access is the Online Computer Library Center (OCLC). This provides a variety of resources including FirstSearch, which contains a series of databases called the WorldCat (titles of books, journals and manuscripts), Article1st (titles of articles in academic journals) and NetFirst (material accessible via the World Wide Web). OCLC is only available through libraries that subscribe to it, not to private individuals, but it is well worth checking whether your library can give you access to it.

Some on-line catalogues contain only works published after a certain date, so while they may be good for recent scholarship, they may be no help at all with anything earlier. So check what kind of coverage a bibliographical database gives before you waste time trying to find a text that simply isn't there.

Using the World Wide Web

Some basics

If you are uncertain of the basic terminology or have no knowledge of the Internet, you would be well advised to consult one of the books mentioned in the bibliography at the end of this chapter. My purpose here is to offer advice that will enable you to use information technology intelligently and discriminatingly. It is very easy to be charmed by the power and seductive attractions of the Internet. It is less easy to use the wonderful resource it offers to its maximum advantage.

The following explanations of basic terms are given merely to clarify the terminology used in this chapter:

The Internet is a collection of computer networks that operate throughout the world. It is based on a common global understanding among computer and software designers about the way that communication systems should be designed. This network of communication devices has enormous potential. The two most widely used facilities of the Internet are the World Wide Web and e-mail.

The World Wide Web (the Web/WWW) is a vast, easily-navigable collection of information held on many of the computers that are connected by the Internet. This information may include text, graphics, audio files and video clips, as well as links to other pages or sites.

Electronic Mail (e-mail) is also carried by the Internet. It differs from the World Wide Web in that it is designed to enable individuals or groups of people to communicate directly with each other. In order to use e-mail you have to have an e-mail address (looking something like <wamozart@vienna.org>). It is not necessary to have an e-mail address to use the Web, but most people who use the Web also use e-mail.

A World Wide Web site is the place or address on the Web where the documents, graphics and sounds made available by an individual or organization are found. The first thing you see when you get to a site is the opening page or 'homepage' of the site. Pages can be connected to each other by hypertext links (highlighted words or images) that transfer you to a different page of the site. Sites usually also contain links to completely different sites. Many Web sites are available to everyone free of charge, but others are not, and it is necessary to subscribe to them and pay a fee in order to obtain a password that will give you access. Other sites or parts of sites may also be 'password-protected' because, for example, they are reserved for registered students or staff of a particular institution. However, some of the most helpful and comprehensive sites (such as those of most major libraries) are entirely free.

Browsers are computer programmes that allow you to access World Wide Web sites. These browser programmes also allow you to print out pages, and download information to your computer. The two most widely used browsers are Netscape and Microsoft Internet Explorer.

Search engines are free Web sites which act as directories for most or all of the millions of other sites. You can use search engines to find sites by using keywords or some other broad descriptor of what you are looking for. Searching on the word 'Mozart', for example, would yield any site that makes prominent use of the word 'Mozart' –

including chocolate factories, tourist agencies and advertisements for publications about the music of W. A. Mozart. Two of the most popular search engines are Yahoo! and Alta Vista. However, there are yet more effective meta-search engines, and these are described below.

Knowing good from bad

Much of the information that is available in libraries is also available on the Internet. But there are distinct differences between the sources held in libraries and those accessed via the Internet. Books need to be published and distributed, and these processes usually ensure that they receive careful scrutiny. This does not mean that all published books are of equal authority or quality, or even that all of them are entirely trustworthy. But books published by the most respected academic publishers are scrutinized and re-scrutinized before they are seen by the general public. The likelihood that totally bogus information could become widely circulated through them is relatively small. On the other hand, anyone can launch a Web site at any time on any subject, without that site ever being scrutinized for its value, quality, accuracy or even its decency. The Web has sites that are comprehensive and authoritative, adhering to the highest ethical and scholarly standards. It also has an abundance of unvetted rubbish that displays itself self-confidently as serious comment. So how do you know what is good and reliable and what is not so good?

Many people who search the Internet for information do so by using one of the major search engines. You search by asking the search engine to find those sites that contain a particular keyword. For example, the keyword 'Handel' produces more than half a million 'hits' (results) in the Alta Vista search engine. It is then possible to access any or all of these sites to see what they contain. The challenge comes in determining which of these half-million sites are relevant. Amending the search term to 'George Frideric Handel' reduces the number of hits significantly: out go the florists, trinket makers and haulage firms that have 'Handel' in their title or trading particulars. But there are still 37,000 hits left. They will include advertisements for modern publications of the works of Handel, the sites of individual Handel enthusiasts, sales pitches for Handel replica memorabilia and, amidst all this, the sites that refer to some of the most important focuses for scholarship and literature on Handel.

If your approach is entirely speculative, you could waste a great deal of time and end up with bogus information. It is important to have a strategy that allows you (at least initially) to find sites you can trust. An Internet site that is helpful and can be depended on should have the following important qualities:

• It must be relevant to your needs.
• It must be authoritative and reliable.
• It should be easy to use and provide links to other relevant sites.
• It must be regularly serviced and updated.

The question of relevance is a difficult one to deal with in a book such as this because of the vast array of possible topics for research projects. But the key to finding really relevant and trustworthy information on the Web is, in many cases, to use it as just *one* of your research resources. The process of determining reliable and relevant information might well originate in the scrutiny of printed material.

Some of the most reliable Web sites are found through the recommendation of teachers or through publications that give evaluations of such sites. But if you are approaching this fresh and want to assure yourself that a site is trustworthy and accurate, it is worth considering some key questions about a site:

• Who authored it, and for what reason? Some sites are set up for no reason other than to provide information. Others are set up to persuade you to buy something, or to persuade you to a particular view or ideology. Some are created as a hobby or pastime, to entertain, or merely so that an individual or group of people can make information about themselves public. Some are primarily the outlet for vanity. How do you determine the motives that lie behind a site, and how do you then test whether it has the qualities you are looking for? The following further questions are helpful in this respect.
• Does an official, legal or properly regulated authority (such as a university, government agency or library) take responsibility for the site? The sites of most universities, for example, include disclaimers stating that they cannot vouch for the accuracy of all the information that is linked to their site. This is indeed true, but the institutions are as reliable as you can get, and the disclaimers themselves are evidence of a culture of responsibility.
• Would the owners of a particular site stand to lose anything by

way of reputation or credibility if the information on their site were to be regarded as disreputable or inaccurate?

- Conversely, is the owner of the site – whether it be an individual, an institution or an agency – known nationally or internationally for its quality and authority?
- Do other well-known national agencies or institutions show their faith in a particular site by providing links to it from their own site?

Not every reliable site would have *all* these qualities, but most should have *some* of them. An initial impression of the type of organization that has set up the site can be gained from looking at its address as it is revealed in its URL (Uniform Resource Locator).

The URL contains information that provides the signals your computer needs to enter the Web. Usually the URL begins <http://www>. (The angle brackets enclosing these letters are not part of the URL. They are simply a convention used in written text to mark off e-mail and Web site addresses from the words that surround them. See page 96.) The address contains information about the owner or 'host' of the site. It also contains a 'domain' name, which will tell you whether the host is an educational institution, a commercial organization and so on. For example, an address that contains the code <.ac.uk> is short for 'academic United Kingdom', which means that it is a UK educational institution (see Fig. 3.4); <.au.edu> means 'Australia education', indicating that it too is an educational institution. Every country has a code (though it need not always be used). For example:

au	Australia	jp	Japan
ca	Canada	my	Malaysia
de	Germany	nz	New Zealand
fr	France	sg	Singapore
hk	Hong Kong	uk	United Kingdom

Usually (but not invariably) an address that does not carry a country code means that the host is in the USA; for example <.edu> without an indicator of country means a United States educational institution. These are the most common domain types:

ac	Academic institution or agency in the UK
com	Company or commercial organization

co   Company or commercial organization in the UK
edu   Educational institution
gov   Government body or agency
mil   Military agency
net   Internet gateway
org   Non-profit making or non-commercial organization

These codes can provide indicators of the motive and status of a site host, but you should not draw rigid conclusions from them. Many <.com> hosts are extremely authoritative and responsible, and not all <.ac> or <.edu> sites operate to the high and exacting standards that are observed by others.

More advanced Web searches

A good search engine could also help you eliminate at least some irrelevant sites. There is a type of search engine that performs 'meta-searches', which means that it gets its results by searching a number of other search engines such as Alta Vista and Yahoo!. These meta-search engines are usually fast, and the best give you a sophisticated range of options for 'filtering' information before it reaches you. This means that an engine will be selective in what it finds for you. For example, some will allow you not only to specify that you want to be informed of sites that match your keyword(s), but also that you want to find sites in '.ac' and '.edu' domains, but do *not* want to be informed of sites in other domains. Meta-search engines save you time and allow you to look for sites much more efficiently. Some of the best are given below; it is worth testing them all out with the same set of keywords to see which suits you best:

<www.google.com>
<www.alltheweb.com>
<www.northernlight.com>
<www.dogpile.com>
<www.mamma.com>

The list of research and reference works in Chapter 8 includes a number of Web sites that are helpful and regularly updated. In the case of universities, the hosts have set up their Web sites in such a way as to guide their own students to pathways that are sound and

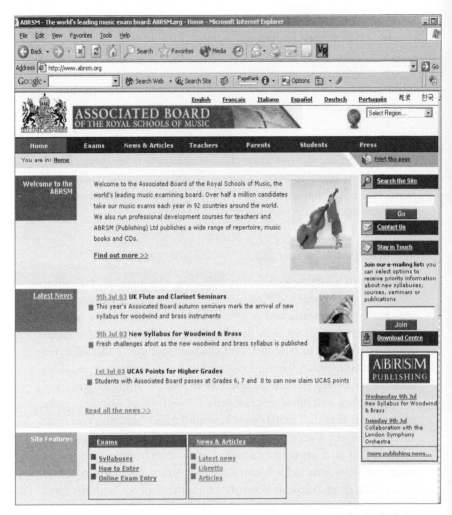

Fig. 3.4   The homepage of the Associated Board of the Royal Schools of Music. Here, the URL (<www.abrsm.org>) is given towards the bottom of the page, below the e-mail address. Words that are underlined are links to other pages or sites. The site also has a 'quick search' facility.

reliable. These sites will be helpful in their own right, but they can also be seen as models of their type. The *Music in Words* Web page <http://www.abrsmpublishing.co.uk/musicinwords> provides links to the sites mentioned in this book and to some other useful Web addresses.

Bibliography

Library directories

Aslib (Association for Information Management) Web site:
<http://www.aslib.co.uk>

Dale, P. (ed.), *Directory of Museum and Special Collections in the United Kingdom*, 2nd edn (London: Aslib, 1996).

Reynard, K. W., and J. M. E. Reynard (eds), *Aslib Directory of Information Sources in the United Kingdom*, 2 vols (London: Aslib [published biennially]). Also on CD-ROM.

World Guide to Libraries, 14th edn (Munich: Saur, 1999). Also available on-line by subscription.

World Guide to Special Libraries, 4th edn (Munich: Saur, 1998). Also available on-line by subscription as *World Guide to Libraries Plus*.

See also:

Hoffmann, A., *Research for Writers*, 6th edn (London: A. & C. Black, 1999), Chapter 3.

The Internet

Books about the Internet go out of date very quickly, so do not regard this list as definitive. Also check Internet guides that are actually on the Internet, such as the BBC's Webwise site (see below).

BBC Education Webwise site: <http://www.bbc.co.uk/webwise/>

Dorner, J., *The Internet: A Writer's Guide* (London: A. & C. Black, 2000).

Fielden, N. L., and M. Garrido, *Internet Research: Theory and Practice* (Jefferson, N. Carolina; London: McFarland & Co., Inc., 1998).

Kennedy, A. J., *The Internet: The Rough Guide* (London: Rough Guides Ltd [regularly updated]). Web site: <http://www.roughguides.com>

Chapter four

SCHOLARLY CONVENTIONS: CITING SOURCES

THIS CHAPTER contains an explanation of what 'scholarly conventions' or 'citation conventions' are, why they exist, and why it is desirable in certain types of academic writing for there to be a system for using them that is commonly understood and shared among authors and readers. This chapter is linked to Chapters 9, 10 and 11 in Part II, which provide illustrations of the main citation conventions for different types of source. Each chapter is devoted to one category of sources: Chapter 9 to 'The printed word' – that is, books, scholarly articles, newspapers and so on; Chapter 10 to 'Musical sources', which includes the citation of different musical genres, as well as recorded music; and Chapter 11 to 'Other sources', including paintings, films, oral interview material and Web pages.

Citation (sometimes called 'referencing') is the means by which you identify books and other material you have used in your own writing. There is more than one way of citing sources (this is particularly noticeable with the printed word, as I explain below), and as you read the works of other writers you will undoubtedly notice that their citation methods differ – for example, in the way a citation is punctuated. So it is not my intention to give either a single definitive system for each type of source or a comprehensive breakdown of all the possible methods and their variations, but simply to provide models that are clear, correct and acceptable.

Why citations and scholarly conventions are used

Music researchers investigate musical topics, find new information and publish books and articles about it. Thus all well researched and well presented musical scholarship contributes to our knowledge of music. It is as if there were an on-going public debate about music and musical practices in which the participants continually add information for the common good of all who are taking part – and anyone can take part. However, fundamental to that debate is the sharing not only of views and conclusions, but also of factual information about the evidence on which those views and conclusions are based. The sources used by the writer must, therefore, be open and apparent to the reader.

So how do you ensure that your sources are clear to your reader? As I have said, a source can be anything – a book, a newspaper article, a score, a performance, an interview, a film, or whatever – from which you quote or to which you refer in your own writing. When you quote from or refer to a source, you must show that you have done so by acknowledging it and providing its details. You do this for two reasons:

- to give due credit to the person or persons who created the source that you are using;
- to provide information for your readers that will enable them to trace your sources and see whether they share the conclusions you have drawn from them. In effect, any piece of research should contain comprehensive information about how the research has been conducted. It should enable others to repeat the research you have done, in order to see whether you have worked accurately and drawn your conclusions justifiably.

This sharing of information can only work effectively if there are common systems for identifying sources, and if the systems contain all the information a reader needs in order to find those sources. Whether a source is a book, a manuscript, a TV programme or any one of the multitude of items that scholars draw on, there is an accepted format – or *convention* – for identifying it in writing.

If you are writing an academic essay or article for which formal academic citations are appropriate, you need to use citations to acknowledge your sources in the following circumstances:

- if you are using an actual quotation from another source;
- if you are paraphrasing another source;
- if you are referring directly to another source;
- if your own writing is closely based on, or is drawn heavily from, the work of another writer;
- if you wish, for some other reason, to draw attention to a source.

It is important to emphasize that citations must be identified with

absolute accuracy. If any detail is given wrongly, it could make it difficult or even impossible for others to trace your sources.

Plagiarism

I have placed an explanation of plagiarism alongside my explanation
of citations with good reason, because plagiarism acts against open-
ness and honesty in scholarship. Plagiarism is an attempt to pass off
the writings of others as one's own work – by copying directly or by
paraphrasing – without acknowledging it. Most schools, universities
and examination agencies have rules that warn students against
plagiarism. Everyone uses the writings of others to inform their own
work, but the process of acknowledging such borrowings is simple,
courteous and ultimately helpful.

Bibliographies

I want to start by looking at the way to cite written sources such as
books and academic journals, because this is fundamental to all good
academic writing procedures. If you become familiar with the citation
methods for printed sources, it provides a solid foundation for
research and writing.

There are two aspects to the citation of printed sources:
• the notes (footnotes, endnotes or in-text references – these are
  explained and illustrated below), in which you acknowledge
  quotations from or references to the works of other writers;
• the bibliography (sometimes called a list of references), which
  usually appears at the end of an essay or book, and in which you
  give the full details of the written sources you have used.

This chapter describes two commonly used citation methods for
printed sources: the short-title system and the author–date system.
For each system a particular style of note goes hand-in-hand with a
particular style of bibliography. If you are not required to use either
one system or the other (by a publisher or examiner, for example) you
can choose which you wish to use. However, the golden rule is that,
throughout a piece of writing, you must adhere consistently to the
style you have chosen. By being consistent, you help your reader to
understand what you intend to convey.

You need to understand bibliographies, because, as well as needing to draw up the bibliography for your own project, you will encounter bibliographical citations in library catalogues (see Chapter 3) and in the bibliographies of the works of other writers.

A bibliography is a list of books and other printed sources. It does not usually contain citations of other types of source such as pictures or personal letters and e-mails you have received – these are cited as footnotes or endnotes, or in brackets in your written text as you go along. Archived manuscript sources and Web sites, on the other hand, should be cited in your bibliography, while recorded music is cited separately, under a discography. Chapters 10 and 11 deal with the citation conventions for these other types of sources.

Together, the notes and bibliography form the system that allows readers to trace and check sources, and to follow them up. Your bibliography should include not just the sources you quote from or refer to, but also any that significantly influenced your writing, even if you do not quote from or refer to them directly.

Whereas the purpose of notes is to signal the points in a text where you have used specific sources, the purpose of the bibliography is to give complete details (*bibliographical* details) of publications and other sources in a way that will allow readers to track them down in library catalogues. For this to work efficiently, it is necessary for a bibliography to give the same information about, say, a book as is given in library catalogues. Consequently, all bibliographical citations require standard pieces of information (see page 72 below, 'Where to find the bibliographical details of a book'). However, the order in which the information is given will vary depending on whether you use the short-title system (Fig. 4.1) or the author–date system (Fig. 4.2). The citation in both cases should include:

- the name of the author or editor of the work;
- the title of the work;
- the title of any larger work of which it is a part, and the name of the editor of this larger work (for example, you may have looked at a chapter of a book to which a number of people have contributed);
- the volume number or series title (if there is one);
- the edition number if it is not the first edition;
- the place of publication and the name of the publisher (if the place of publication is part of the publisher's name – as with the

University of Chicago Press or Oxford University Press – there is no need to give the place as well; if the town or city is not well known, you should also give the country or, for the USA, the state);
- the date of publication.

The sources listed in a bibliography are given in alphabetical order of writers' or editors' surnames. If the author's name is not known, use the abbreviation 'Anon.' for 'Anonymous', and list the book under 'A'. If the publication is produced by an institution rather than a named person – for example, by a museum, or for an exhibition or concert – it should be listed in the alphabetical sequence under the initial letter of the first major word of the title ('A', 'An' and 'The' are not regarded as major words).

If you wish to list more than one work by the same author or editor, there is no need to repeat the author's name each time. Instead, you can replace the name with a long dash like this: —— . If some of the works are written or edited jointly with another person, the other person's name should follow the dash.

Two abbreviations that you may come across or need to use are 'n.d.' and 'n.p.'.
- 'n.d.' means 'no date' or 'not dated', and is used when the date of a publication is not known. If the date is known (for example, from another source), but not printed on the publication, give the date, but enclose it in square brackets.
- 'n.p.' means 'no place of publication', and is used when the place of publication is not known. If the place is known from another source, again, put it in square brackets.

These abbreviations are most commonly required when you are dealing with books published before the twentieth century. The publication details of modern books are usually more standardized and much more comprehensive.

Bibliographies are sometimes sub-categorized so that, for example, there is a list of published books, a list of periodicals (such as journals and newspapers), a list of the private papers or manuscripts consulted and so on.

(1) Andrews, M. (ed.), Musical Style (Sydney: Academic Press, 1995).

(2) Anon., New Instructions for the Orchestral Conductor (London: Best (3) & Co., 1861).

Anon., Best's Violin Primer (London: Best & Co., 1901).

David, J.–F., Mémoires de l'orchestre (Paris: Éditions Apollon, (4) n.d.).

Graham, K., The Orchestra in the British Empire (Auckland: D. H. Davies, 1980).

James, G. W., Woodwind Technique (New York: Music Education Press, 1925).

(5) The Melbourne Festiva l 1928: Souvenir Programme (Melbourne: Thomas & Sons, 1928). (6)

Morris, T., Letters Home from the Orient (n.p., 1922).

Peters, M., and L. Martin (eds), Orchestr a 2000, The (7) International Orchestra Yearbook (London: Musicians Press, 2000).

Roberts, P., 'The earliest orchestral recordings: a source for (8) performance analysts', Journal of Performing Traditions, 21 (1989), 22–48. (9)

Slater, G., The Orchestra in the Twentieth Century, 2 vols (10) (London: Whiting Press, 1962).

(11) —, 'The twentieth-century orchestra revisited' in P. Gunnet (ed.), Essays on Orchestral Performance (New York: Barker Press, 2000), pp. 130–45. (12)

—, A History of Musical Criticism 1700–2000, 2nd edn (London: D. W. Brown, 2000). (13)

(14) — and J. Thompson (eds.), Orchestral Performance Practice in the Twentieth Century (London: James & Macintosh, 1982).

Thomas, T., The Recording Engineer's Guide: A Manual for Studio Recordings (Edinburgh: Nonpardy Press, 1955).

Unwin-Porter, R., My Life with the Bass Trombone (Chiswick: Small Press, 1949).

Fig. 4.1 **Bibliography (short-title system)**

Bibliographies are organized in alphabetical order of authors' surnames (so you should put the surname first).

(1) M. Andrews is the editor rather than the author of this book.

(2) The names of the authors of these books are not known, so they are listed under 'Anon.' ('Anonymous').

(3) If a publisher uses an ampersand (&) in its name rather than the word 'and', you should do the same.

(4) The date of this book is not known, so 'n.d.' ('not dated') is put in its place.

The two major citation systems

The short-title system and the author–date system have their origins in different areas of scholarship: the short-title system (also known as the humanities or documentary-note system) is traditional in arts and humanities writing; the author–date system originates in the sciences. However, both have gained a wider currency, and both are equally effective and in equally common use. Irrespective of which system you use, it is worth familiarizing yourself with both, because you will encounter both in your reading and research about music.

In this chapter, I explain the two systems using a book as my example. I deal first with the way a book is cited in a bibliography, according to each system. I then deal with how a book is cited in notes, according to each system. The way that other publications – such as journal articles, chapters, subsequent editions of books and so on – are cited is illustrated in Chapter 9.

Bibliographical systems

THE SHORT-TITLE SYSTEM

The term 'short-title' refers to the style of notes rather than the bibliography. The system works like this:

Fig. 4.1   *continued*

⑤ This book is by an institution rather than a named person, so it is listed under 'M', the first letter of the first main word of the title.

⑥ The place of publication of this book is not known, so 'n.p.' ('no place of publication') is put in its place.

⑦ This book is part of an annual series, so it has both a book title (in italics) and a series title (in roman).

⑧ This is an article in a journal; the article title is given in roman and quotes, and the *journal title* is given in italics.

⑨ The page range is also given, but the abbreviation 'pp.' ('pages') is omitted because this is a journal article.

⑩ This book is in two volumes.

⑪ This chapter is also by G. Slater; the dash shows that the name is repeated.

⑫ This is the page range of the chapter; unlike journal articles, the abbreviation 'pp.' is used.

⑬ This is the second edition of the book.

⑭ This book is edited by both G. Slater and J. Thompson. (The works an author wrote alone are listed first, followed by any multi-authored works.)

Andrews, M. (ed.). 1995. Musical Style. Sydney: Academic Press.

Anon. 1861. New Instructions for the Orchestral Conductor. London: Best & Co.

Anon. 1901. Best's Violin Primer. London: Best & Co.

David, J.–F. n.d. Mémoires de l'orchestre. Paris: Éditions Apollon.

Graham, K. 1980. The Orchestra in the British Empire. Auckland: D. H. Davies.

James, G. W. 1925. Woodwind Technique. New York: Music Education Press.

The Melbourne Festival 1928: Souvenir Programme. 1928. Melbourne: Thomas & Sons.

Morris, T. 1922. Letters Home from the Orient. n.p.

Peters, M., and L. Martin (eds). 2000. Orchestra 2000. The International Orchestra Yearbook. London: Musicians Press.

Roberts, P. 1989. The earliest orchestral recordings: a source for performance analysts. Journal of Performing Traditions, 21: 22–48.

Slater, G. 1962. The Orchestra in the Twentieth Century, 2 vols. London: Whiting Press.

— 2000a. The twentieth-century orchestra revisited. In P. Gunnet (ed.), Essays on Orchestral Performance, pp. 130–45. New York: Barker Press.

— 2000b. A History of Musical Criticism 1700–2000. 2nd edn. London: D. W. Brown.

— and J. Thompson (eds.). 1982. Orchestral Performance Practice in the Twentieth Century. London: James & Macintosh.

Thomas, T. 1955. The Recording Engineer's Guide: A Manual for Studio Recordings. Edinburgh: Nonpardy Press.

Unwin-Porter, R. 1949. My Life with the Bass Trombone. Chiswick: Small Press.

Fig. 4.2   **Bibliography (author–date system)**

This bibliography contains the same information as in Fig. 4.1, but uses the author–date system. I have picked out the main differences.

1. Unlike the short-title system, the date immediately follows the author's or editor's name and full stops are generally used to separate the elements (apart from place of publication and publisher).

2. Article and chapter titles are not put in quotes.

3. The volume number is separated from the page number(s) by a colon.

4. When the list contains more than one work by the same author, published in the same year, distinguish between them by calling one 'a', the next 'b' and so on.

- a full bibliographical citation is given the first time a book (or other source) is mentioned in a note;
- in subsequent citations a shortened form of the title is used (see Fig. 4.3, point (2), page 68 below).

In the short-title system, the elements of the citation for a book in a bibliography are given in the following order:
- name of the author or editor (surname first);
- book title (in italics);
- place of publication, publisher's name and publication date (all inside round brackets).

For example:

> Andrews, M. (ed.), *Musical Style* (Sydney: Academic Press, 1995).

> Slater, G., *The Orchestra in the Twentieth Century*, 2 vols (London: Whiting Press, 1962).

It is important that you are consistent in the way you punctuate the citation. Mine is not the definitive model, but it is a common one. The author or editor's name is separated from the book title by a comma, and, in the second example, a comma also separates the book title from the number of volumes. However, there is no punctuation immediately before the round bracket that contains the publication details. Within the bracket, the place of publication and the publisher's name are separated by a colon, and the date is preceded by a comma.

It does not usually matter whether you give the author or editor's full first name or just the initial(s), but since some writers choose to use their initials rather than their first names, it is usually easiest to give initials for everybody in your bibliography, for the sake of consistency.

THE AUTHOR–DATE SYSTEM

The author–date system (also known as the Harvard system) is so called because the information in both bibliography and note is set out so as to give prominence to the author's surname and the date of publication. Each bibliographical citation should contain the following elements, in this order:
- name of the author or editor (surname first);

- date of publication;
- book title (in italics);
- place of publication;
- publisher.

For example:

Andrews, M. (ed.). 1995. *Musical Style.* Sydney: Academic Press.

Slater, G. 1962. *The Orchestra in the Twentieth Century.* 2 vols. London: Whiting Press.

In the author–date bibliography, most elements of the citation are separated from each other by a full stop, apart from the place of publication and publisher's name, which are separated by a colon. It is worth looking again at Figs 4.1 and 4.2 and comparing the formats for bibliographical citations in the two systems. This will help you recognize their different features.

How to cite sources in text: as footnotes, endnotes or in-text references?

Bibliographies provide the fullest details of your sources, but in scholarly writing it is not sufficient simply to *list* all the sources that you have consulted. You have to acknowledge which sources you have used at different points in your work. It would interrupt the flow if you were to give the full bibliographical details every time you mentioned a source, so conventions exist that enable you to do this properly and unobtrusively.

Of course, rather than simply using a note or in-text reference, you may want to include a broad acknowledgement to a particular work within the main body of your writing, and it is a good idea to acknowledge a work on which you have relied heavily in this more conspicuous way.

For example:

It is immaterial whether one likes or dislikes popular music. The real issue is that it should receive special attention by musicologists, and should be scrutinized using appropriate analytical methods. This view is based substantially on the argument put forward by Richard Middleton in *Studying Popular Music* (1990).

This conspicuous reference to Richard Middleton's book helps to underline its importance to the debate that is being discussed here; but so as not to interrupt the flow of the argument, the full bibliographical citation would be given in your bibliography.

In many other instances, however, you will simply want to point your readers to a specific book or article from which you have drawn a quotation or reference. How you do this will depend on whether you choose to use the short-title or the author–date system.

USING NOTES IN THE SHORT-TITLE SYSTEM

In the short-title system, a number placed immediately after a quotation signals a footnote or endnote. Footnotes and endnotes do the same thing; they are just put in different places:

- footnotes are placed at the bottom (the foot) of the page to which they are relevant;
- endnotes are placed together, either at the end of each chapter or article, or at the end of the book.

Word-processor programmes make footnoting and endnoting easy.

Fig. 4.3 shows the system in practice (footnotes are used here, but the same principle applies to endnotes – they would be at the end of the piece, rather than at the bottom of the page).

The first time you cite a source, you cite it in full and include the number of the page you are quoting from or referring to, as shown in footnote 2 in Fig. 4.3. (In contrast to the bibliography, here the author's first name or initial comes first.) If you need to cite this book again, as in footnote 6, you need only use a shortened version of the citation. In the body of the main text the footnote number comes after any punctuation such as a comma, full stop or closing quotation mark, and is usually printed as superscript or enclosed in brackets. But remember that the *full* bibliographical citation will appear not only in the first mention of the book, but also in your bibliography.

There are occasions, as you can see in footnote 4 in Fig. 4.3, when you may choose to use a note to explain something that you write in the main text, because you do not wish to disturb the flow of the argument – but don't do this too often. A well-constructed argument should not need a lot of qualifying notes.

Early recordings show how distinctive the orchestras of different countries sounded at the start of the twentieth century. Slater identified the factors that eventually led to a more uniform sound in the early 1960s.[2] But the full impact of this globalisation was not apparent even by then. It was in the last thirty years of the century that the pace of standardisation quickened. So what caused this standardisation: what led to the 'monotonous global sameness' that Slater later described?[3]

New technologies observe no territorial boundaries. The lines of CDs stacked in record stores in the USA are similar to those in European stores. Radio broadcasts are equally ubiquitous. Orchestras have toured since the earliest decades of the century, but it is the mobility of conductors, the mediators of orchestral style, that has been most influential. As the century progressed, an elite set have travelled the globe, some holding key posts on different continents simultaneously.[4] It has been argued that this aspect of cross-fertilisation has emphasised distinctiveness rather than difference:

> ...at the Salzburg Festival [in 1976] I heard the Berlin Philharmonic perform the 'Pastoral' Symphony with Rzmenski conducting. A month later, I heard the LSO play it at the Proms with the same conductor. The two performances were *utterly* different. It was not just that the orchestral timbres were different, but that these very differences seemed to have acted on Rzmenski's interpretation.[5]

But most commentators observe a dilution of difference that is malignant, and will lead to a monolithic 'global sound', eventually and inevitably matching nothing other than itself. The orchestral sounds (I use the plural deliberately) known to composers writing before 1950 will vanish without trace. Yet more worrying is the possibility that what Slater called 'an expectation of correctness'[6] will develop. There will be but one way that the listening public, and more important the conductors and recording engineers that stand between them and orchestral players, will find acceptable.

Of course, a similar phenomenon can be witnessed in any small-town high street. Local traders, small shops and restaurants have vanished, to be replaced by the familiar signs of the multi-nationals and the ubiquitous Macdonald's. In the 1950s the urban landscape was marked by the shop fronts of local traders. At the end of the century you could open your eyes after arriving in a small town, and you could be anywhere.

1. See P. Roberts, 'The earliest orchestral recordings: a source for performance analysts', *Journal of Performing Traditions*, 21 (1989), 22–48.
2. G. Slater, *The Orchestra in the Twentieth Century*, Vol. 1 (London: Whiting Press, 1962), pp. 82–3.
3. G. Slater, 'The twentieth-century orchestra revisited' in Gunnet, P. (ed.), *Essays on Orchestral Performance* (New York: Barker Press, 2000), p. 137.
4. For example, Pierre Boulez was principal conductor of the New York Philharmonic from 1971–8 and of the BBC Symphony Orchestra from 1971–4.
5. Quoted in G. Slater, *A History of Musical Criticism 1700–2000* (London: D. W. Brown, 2000), p. 99.
6. Slater, *Orchestra*, Vol. 2, p. 55.

USING CITATIONS IN THE AUTHOR–DATE SYSTEM

The author–date system uses an 'in-text reference': that is, a citation in brackets immediately after the quotation from or reference to a work (Fig. 4.4). As you can see, there is no note number, just a round bracket containing the author's surname and the publication date, and, where neccessary, a page reference, which is separated from the rest of the information by a comma. (It is common in this system for the 'p.' abbreviation for 'page', or 'pp.' for 'pages', to be left out.) If a particular volume needs to be cited, the volume number precedes the page number and is separated from it by a colon. The full citation is given in a bibliography at the end of the piece.

In the example shown in Fig. 4.4 the writer has used several works by G. Slater, two of which were published in 2000. In the short-title system this is not a problem, because you would always cite either the full title of each work or a shortened version of it, so it would always be distinguishable from other works by the same author, even if several are published in the same year. But in the author–date system you cannot refer to several publications by the same in-text reference such as '(Slater 2000)'. So you must distinguish between them, and the way to do this is to call one work '2000a', the next '2000b' and so on, as the writer has done in Fig. 4.4. (You must then, of course, be careful also to list the works *in the bibliography* under '2000a' and '2000b'.)

The author–date system of in-text references clearly does not let you insert additional information in the way that foot- or endnotes do. As with the short-title system, you should think carefully about whether you really need such additional explanations, and, if you do, keep them to a minimum. If you add such information to the main body of your writing, foot- or endnotes may be used in addition to the author–date in-text references. The writer has done this with footnote 1 in Fig. 4.4.

Fig. 4.3   *(Left)* **Footnotes and the short-title system**

(1) A number at the appropriate point in the text indicates the footnote. The footnote number comes *after* any punctuation.

(2) The first time a work is mentioned (footnote 2), the full bibliographical citation is given, together with the specific page reference. The second time (footnote 6), the bibliographical citation is shortened.

(3) Sometimes a footnote can be used to give information that is incidental to the main argument.

Early recordings show how distinctive the orchestras of different countries sounded at the start of the twentieth century (Roberts 1989, 22–48). Slater identified the factors that eventually led to a more uniform sound in the early 1960s (Slater 1962, 1: 82–3). But the full impact of this globalisation was not apparent even by then. It was in the last thirty years of the century that the pace of standardisation quickened. So what caused this standardisation: what led to the 'monotonous global sameness' that Slater later described? (Slater 2000a, 137)

New technologies observe no territorial boundaries. The lines of CDs stacked in record stores in the USA are similar to those in European stores. Radio broadcasts are equally ubiquitous. Orchestras have toured since the earliest decades of the century, but it is the mobility of conductors, the mediators of orchestral style, that has been most influential. As the century progressed, an elite set have travelled the globe, some holding key posts on different continents simultaneously.[1] It has been argued that this aspect of cross-fertilisation has emphasised distinctiveness rather than difference:

> ...at the Salzburg Festival [in 1976] I heard the Berlin Philharmonic perform the 'Pastoral' Symphony with Rzmenski conducting. A month later, I heard the LSO play it at the Proms with the same conductor. The two performances were *utterly* different. It was not just that the orchestral timbres were different, but that these very differences seemed to have acted on Rzmenski's interpretation. (Slater 2000b, 99)

But most commentators observe a dilution of difference that is malignant, and will lead to a monolithic 'global sound', eventually and inevitably matching nothing other than itself. The orchestral sounds (I use the plural deliberately) known to composers writing before 1950 will vanish without trace. Yet more worrying is the possibility that what Slater called 'an expe tation of correctness' (Slater 1962, 2: 55) will develop. There will be but one way that the listening public, and more important the conductors and recording engineers that stand between them and orchestral players, will find acceptable.

Of course, a similar phenomenon can be witnessed in any small-town high street. Local traders, small shops and restaurants have vanished, to be replaced by the familiar signs of the multi-nationals and the ubiquitous Macdonald's. In the 1950s the urban landscape was marked by the shop fronts of local traders. At the end of the century you could open your eyes after arriving in a small town, and you could be anywhere.

---

[1]   For example, Pierre Boulez was principal conductor of the New York Philharmonic from 1971–8 and of the BBC Symphony Orchestra from 1971–4.

Fig. 4.4   **The author–date system**

(1) A reference to the work in question is given in brackets in the text (an in-text reference). This gives the author's surname and date of publication, and, if appropriate, a precise page reference (the abbreviation 'p.' for 'page' can be omitted).

QUOTING A QUOTATION

If you quote a piece of text that is already a quotation in the source that you are using, you should acknowledge this in your note or in-text reference with the phrase 'Quoted in' (see Fig. 4.5). As you can see, the passage below contains a quotation of something that Svenson said. However, the writer's source is a quotation of Svenson's words from a book by J. Dickens – so the writer acknowledges Dickens, not Svenson.

Over a period of twenty years Svenson's piano technique developed considerably. So did his capacity to work in more than one musical idiom. He often played concerto concerts in the same week as recording a jazz album. He apparently did not find this challenging – quite the contrary in fact: in the later years of his life he said, 'I started playing Beethoven sonatas really well when I became immersed in jazz again. It was as if one idiom refreshed the other.'[3] His extraordinary technique and his ability to cross boundaries of

[3]   Quoted in J. Dickens, *Ten Great Pianists* (Oakdale: Norris Press, 1987), p. 25.

Fig. 4.5   A quotation of a quotation. The author is quoting something that was quoted in another secondary source. The source here is cited as a footnote.

Fig. 4.5 uses the short-title system. In the author–date system (Fig. 4.6) the phrase 'Quoted in' should be added to the in-text reference. (The full reference to Dickens's book would, of course, be given in the bibliography.)

Fig. 4.4   *continued*
(2) The volume number is separated from the page reference by a colon.
(3) If you need to refer to more than one work by the same author, published in the same year, differentiate between them by calling one 'a', the next 'b' and so on.
(4) If a piece of incidental information is needed, a foot- or endnote can be used.

> Over a period of twenty years Svenson's piano technique developed considerably. So did his capacity to work in more than one musical idiom. He often played concerto concerts in the same week as recording a jazz album. He apparently did not find this challenging – quite the contrary in fact: in the later years of his life he said, 'I started playing Beethoven sonatas really well when I became immersed in jazz again. It was as if one idiom refreshed the other.' (Quoted in Dickens 1987, 25.) His extraordinary technique and his ability to cross boundaries of style and period made him one of

Fig. 4.6   A quotation of a quotation. The author is quoting something that was quoted in another secondary source. The source here is cited in an in-text reference.

Where to find the bibliographical details of a book

In Chapters 3 and 8, I discuss library catalogues and bibliographical resources. Apart from enabling you to identify and find a specific book, these resources are also useful for checking the detailed information you need for citations if you don't have the book itself to hand. If you *do* have the book to hand, however, all the information you need will be found on the title page (Fig. 4.7) and the copyright page (Fig. 4.8). These are found just a page or two inside the front cover of the book – the copyright page is usually on the reverse (verso) of the title page.

The copyright page of a modern book contains a great deal of detail, much of it in the form of figures and numerical codes, and standard statements about copyright. In particular, every book published from 1970 onwards has its own unique International Standard Book Number (ISBN), which identifies the country of publication, the publisher and the specific book. It is enormously helpful when you order a book in a bookshop or on interlibrary loan if you can give the ISBN, but ISBNs are not required in the bibliography of an essay or book. Whenever you use a book, however briefly you look at it, you should always turn to the title and copyright pages and make a record of all the details you need for the bibliographical citation (see Chapter 2, page 34).

A COMPANION TO
BEETHOVEN'S
PIANOFORTE SONATAS
(Bar-by-bar Analysis)

DONALD FRANCIS TOVEY

Revised Edition
with Preface and Notes by
BARRY COOPER

THE ASSOCIATED BOARD OF
THE ROYAL SCHOOLS OF MUSIC

Fig. 4.7   A title page.

© Copyright 1931 by The Associated Board of the R.A.M. and the R.C.M.

Revised Edition and New Impression
© Copyright 1998 by The Associated Board of the Royal Schools of Music
14 Bedford Square, London, WC1B 3JG

ISBN 1 86096 086 3

All rights reserved. No part of this book may be reproduced or transmitted in any form or by any means, electronic or mechanical, including photocopying, recording or by any information storage and retrieval system, without permission from the Publisher in writing.

Designed and typeset by Geoffrey Wadsley

Fig. 4.8 A copyright page (usually found on the reverse of the title page).

Bibliography

Butcher, J., *Copy-Editing: The Cambridge Handbook for Editors, Authors and Publishers*, 3rd edn (Cambridge University Press, 1992).

The Chicago Manual of Style, 14th edn (University of Chicago Press, 1993).

Gibaldi, J., *MLA Handbook for Writers of Research Papers*, 4th edn (New York: The Modern Language Association of America, 1995).

Hart's Rules for Compositors and Readers at the University Press, Oxford, 39th edn (Oxford University Press, 1983).

MHRA Style Book, 5th edn (London: The Modern Humanities Research Association, 1996).

Chapter five

USING ILLUSTRATIONS: NOTATED MUSIC, PICTURES, TABLES AND OTHER VISUAL REPRESENTATIONS

ILLUSTRATIONS are used in almost all writings about music. Pictures, diagrams, tables, graphs and music examples can convey essential information in a way that words cannot. In published works such as books, the illustrations are inserted at appropriate points in the text, as and when they are needed. This chapter addresses this 'in-text' approach to incorporating illustrations, but it is not the only satisfactory solution. Essays, dissertations and even book manuscripts can be submitted in two parts: the main text and a supplement – an 'annex' or 'appendix' – that contains all your illustrations. You have to show how the two parts relate to each other, and this chapter explains how this can be done. Most word-processor packages are versatile enough to be able to insert pictures and other 'objects' into written text, but you need good word-processing skills to be able to do this – especially if you use several types of illustration in one piece of writing. So, what is described below applies equally in almost all cases to in-text illustrations and to the main-text-and-supplement model.

Below I deal with the ways in which different types of illustration are handled, but first some more general points need to be considered:

- how you determine whether or not illustrations are necessary or helpful;
- how you signal and label such illustrations so that readers know which one they should be looking at and what its purpose is.

Whether you use one type of illustration or another depends on what you are writing. Music examples may not be a priority for concert programmes aimed at a general audience, because most of the audience will not be able to understand the notation. On the other hand, it is hard to imagine an essay on musical analysis that does not incorporate extensive musical illustrations. Pictures, drawings and other graphic illustrations can proliferate in some publications – for example, in magazine articles they are especially appropriate. But in academic writing they are used much more strategically. Tables – or other lists of data – are especially useful for providing readers with a lot of information in a condensed way. They are also good for clarifying relationships between pieces of information in a way that might be hidden if the data were not in table form.

All these illustrative tools can enhance a piece of writing, but if they are used haphazardly and without due thought they can have the opposite effect: readers can be left wondering why the illustrations are there, what their purpose is and what they are supposed to add to the writing. The subject and purpose of a piece of writing determine the quantity and type of illustrations you use, but most of the following general questions should be asked about any illustration that you are thinking of using.

Is it really necessary?

Most illustrations are used for one or more of the following reasons:
- because they explain or illustrate something for which words are inadequate or less adequate;
- because they present information in a condensed way that is helpful to the reader;
- because they illustrate the subject that is being written about – for example, a person or a musical instrument;
- because they support written text by making it clearer or more convincing;
- because they contain information that is little known or newly discovered, and that is directly relevant to the subject;
- because (in appropriate circumstances) they break up text so as to make it more attractive and palatable. This (as I emphasize below) is the most difficult criterion to determine, and it should be used cautiously in academic writing.

Is the illustration accurate and of adequate visual quality?

If you have decided that the illustrations you wish to use are necessary, it is important to ensure that they are clear and correct. Hence:

- If you are using music examples that are handwritten or produced through a computer notation programme, you must make sure that they are accurate, clear and entirely free of ambiguity.
- Tables can be rendered meaningless if even tiny details are inaccurate, or if the notes and headings that explain them are misleading. They need to be checked carefully.
- If a drawing is used, you should check that the quality of the drawing is good and that what it shows is consistent with the way you describe it. Some technical drawings can make a problem seem more complex rather than clearer.
- Make sure that pictorial or photographic illustrations are well reproduced and that the colours are reasonably true to the original.
- Be sure that you know the context of the illustrations you are using. You must be aware of whether or not a picture is shown in its complete form or whether it is a detail from a larger work, what edition a music example is taken from, and whether quoted tables or other quotations need to have their context clarified.

Are you permitted to use it?

This question mainly applies to writing that is to be published. It is impossible in a book such as this, which is aimed at an international audience, to lay out the circumstances in which it is permissible to use pictures, tables, musical illustrations and quoted text the copyright of which you do not own. The law differs from country to country, and very few generalizations about copyright apply throughout the world. There is a great deal of folklore about copyright, so it is important to obtain accurate information. There are various specialist publications that deal with copyright in detail. A selection is given in the bibliography at the end of this chapter.

Signalling and labelling illustrations

It is essential for a reader to understand why you are using an illustration, and to be able to travel between the main written text and the illustration easily. There are a number of ways to ensure this, but basically illustrations can be unlabelled, following from the text without further identification, or labelled, that is, placed elsewhere in the text or in a supplementary annex, and given an identifier such as 'Example 3' or 'Figure 9'.

Unlabelled illustrations

Sometimes it is appropriate or necessary to introduce a music example at the exact point where it is mentioned. Many didactic (teaching) texts such as those published by the ABRSM show this procedure in use. The passage in Fig. 5.1 from Donald Francis Tovey's book *A Companion to Beethoven's Pianoforte Sonatas* shows how clear this approach can be.

This approach is used more extensively in Eric Taylor's *First Steps in Music Theory* (Fig. 5.2). This type of page set-up is complicated to arrange, but in a publication such as this it is invaluable.

Another example, Fig. 5.3, is taken from *The New Langwill Index*, edited by William Waterhouse. This indispensable reference work includes information about all known makers of Western wind

> closing on to dominant of (V), where 6 bars of dominant prepara-
> tion follow (twice 2 + 1, + 2 confirming chords). As the string-
> quartet version shows, the figure at bars 16/17 is a 2-bar figure
> imitated by another voice, thus:
>
>
>
> **Second Group** in Dominant
> 22/23–30 New 8-bar melody, sequentially answering four (moving
> from B to its supertonic) by 4 a step lower, closing in tonic.
> 30/31–38 Repetition of the melody in inner part with imitations below
> and above.
> 38/39–45 New 4-bar phrase (1 + 1 + 2) with medial close, followed

Fig. 5.1   A music quotation inset and following the flow of the main text.

they are to be played an octave higher or lower (see Grade 1, p. 28). For example,

can be written as

and

can be written as

Fig. 5.2   A series of music quotations inserted into written text.

instruments. The entries are short, like those in a dictionary, so the illustrations of trademarks are incorporated into the appropriate entry without the fuss of further labelling.

Purday, Thomas Edward WWI *fl* London 1835-1865.

ST PAULS CHURCH YD · LONDON · T · E · PURDAY · LATE CLEMENTI & Cᵒ

Music seller, publisher; earlier as BUTTON & PURDAY; *c*1834 took over the music publishing branch of COLLARD & COLLARD; 1835 listed as 'late CLEMENTI & CO.'; inter-relationship with Z.T. PURDAY unknown.

MARK: ST. PAUL'S CHURCH YD. / LONDON / T.E. PURDAY / LATE / CLEMENTI & Co.

Fig. 5.3   A graphic illustration built into the text of a reference book.

Labelled illustrations

In most cases, inserting illustrations at exact points in written text is unnecessary, or difficult. It is particularly difficult to incorporate several such illustrations into home-produced, word-processed writings because of the problems it causes for page breaks. Labelled illustrations can be placed:

- At an exact point in a piece of text in order to illustrate a precise point that is made in the text adjacent to it (even though it and other illustrations in the work are labelled). Short music examples often need to be placed in this way. Publishers often dislike being restricted to placing illustrations at precise points because it limits the flexibility they have to design and set pages.

- At any point in a particular 'opening'. An opening is literally what confronts you when you open a book: the two sides on the left and right of the spine. Usually it is perfectly satisfactory for an illustration to be placed anywhere in the same opening of the text *after* the reference to that illustration. (It is preferable for the reference to an illustration to come before the illustration itself, so that readers can be introduced to the relevance of the illustration before they encounter it.) It is best for music examples to be seen in the same opening as the text that refers to them. The same rule should apply, where possible, to tables.

- At any point in the chapter or section to which it is relevant. Some pictures and photographs need not be placed at precise points in a text, and it is sometimes good for them to be distributed so as to break up the text and give the work an attractive appearance.

- In an annex of examples and illustrations.

Each illustration has an identifier and usually a caption (though captions are not always necessary for music extracts).

The identifier. This is the label that links the illustration to the main text. There are many ways of doing this, but the following method works well. It involves having different sequences for music examples, illustrations and tables:

- Number each music example with an example number (Ex. 1, Ex. 2 and so on).

- Number each table with a table number (Table 1, Table 2 and so on).
- Number all other illustrations (pictures, diagrams and so on) with an illustration number (Ill. 1, Ill. 2 and so on) or a figure number (Fig. 1, Fig. 2 and so on).
- When you mention one of these items in the text, a reference in brackets to the identifier will make clear which illustration you mean. For example:

> Mozart often used short, compact themes repeated at different pitches. The opening of the Symphony K. 201 provides a good example (see Ex. 6).

or

> By the 1960s Armstrong was one of the most famous musicians in the world. Indeed he may have been *the* most famous musician in the world. Press pictures of him with stars such as Frank Sinatra and Dean Martin (see Ill. 10) did much to make him famous even among those who knew nothing of his jazz.

- Use the simplest number sequence that is appropriate: if you have used twenty music examples and twelve other illustrations, the identifiers would be Ex. 1 to Ex. 20 (for extracts of music) and Ill. 1 to Ill. 12 (for other illustrations). This rule obviously applies to essays, articles and other shorter pieces of writing. A useful modification for longer pieces of writing, which saves the necessity of altering every identifier each time you add or withdraw an illustration, is to use a new sequence for each chapter. So, for example, the first music example in Chapter 1 would be identified as Ex. 1.1 and the fifth example in the same chapter would be Ex. 1.5. Similarly the third illustration in Chapter 4 would be Ill. 4.3 and so on.

The caption. Captions can be applied to any illustration provided that there is a need for doing so. It is especially important that pictorial illustrations have captions. The caption should not normally be more than three sentences long and should contain:

- the title of the item that is being illustrated, for example:

> Ill. 3.2. Painting (*c.*1770) of W. A. Mozart, attributed to Saverio dalla Rosa.

- if appropriate, a sentence that explains why the picture is being used (though this is not absolutely necessary);

• a brief acknowledgement to the owner of the copyright of the picture, unless you intend to have a separate list of acknowledgements.

Different types of illustration

Drawings and diagrams

Some illustrations are detailed scale drawings of, for example, the design of auditoriums or musical instruments. Others may not be to scale, but are nevertheless an ideal way of explaining something that would be complicated to describe in words alone. Fig. 5.4 shows the basic principle that makes a valve work on brass instruments.

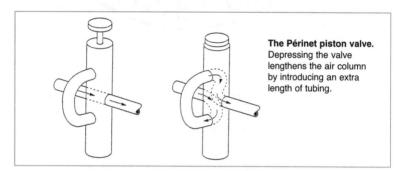

The Périnet piston valve. Depressing the valve lengthens the air column by introducing an extra length of tubing.

Fig. 5.4   Illustration of how valves work on brass instruments, together with the original caption. To explain this process without a diagram would be extremely difficult.

Maps

Maps do not just denote places – they can also show the movements of people between places, demonstrate patterns of change in history, and illustrate other complex issues very clearly (see Fig. 5.5).

Music examples

The presentation of music examples in essays, dissertations and other forms of writing should be consistent and accurate. This section contains advice about the general principles of quoting notated music in written text. Some general points about musical terminology are given in Chapter 7.

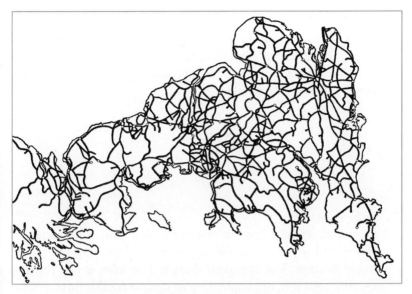

Fig. 5.5
These two maps show the development of railways in the UK. The map on the left shows the network in the 1840s; the map on the right shows how the network was developing in the 1870s. They are used to illustrate the extent to which communication systems developed in England in the nineteenth century, making possible the growth of commercial popular music.

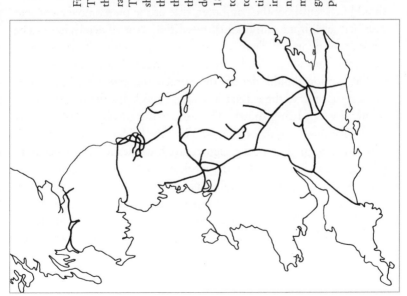

HOW LONG OR SHORT SHOULD AN EXTRACT BE?

A music illustration can be as short as one chord. For example, the famous 'Tristan' chord from Wagner's *Tristan und Isolde* (Ex. 5.1) could be described in terms of pitch names, but on a stave the chord becomes instantly recognizable.

Ex. 5.1

Long music extracts can be expensive and time-consuming to produce, and if you are publishing there could be copyright issues attached to them. The important thing to remember is that you are *illustrating* your text, not duplicating its ideas in another form. Music extracts should only be as long as is necessary for them to make their point effectively.

LABELS AND CAPTIONS FOR MUSIC EXAMPLES

The outline rules given above apply equally to music examples as to other types of illustration. It is essential that the context of the extract should be identified: the composer, title of the piece, movement, bar numbers and (if it is important) the edition. Not all details have to be laboriously quoted if there are successive quotations from the same piece, but movement and bar numbers should always be given.

The caption should identify the extract, and give other brief information that places the extract in context and helps the reader understand why it is being shown. The extract from Robert Philip's book *Early Recordings and Musical Style* (Fig. 5.6) is identified as Ex. 6.18, which means that it is the eighteenth music example to occur in Chapter 6. Philip identifies the work and goes on to illustrate how three different pairs of violinists have used portamento when performing this work by Bach. In the context of what Philip has written about these performances, the illustration is a model of clarity. The illustration is laid out so as to convey information and detail that could not be given using written text alone.

Ex.6.18   J. S. Bach, Concerto in D minor for 2 Violins, second movement, bars 1–16, A. and A. Rosé (on the line), Kreisler and Zimbalist (above the line), and Busch and Magnes (below the line).

Fig. 5.6   Illustration showing a full caption and some additional information superimposed on to the music text. (Our illustration shows bars 1–5 only.)

COMMENTS SUPERIMPOSED ON MUSIC EXTRACTS

Fig. 5.6 is a good illustration of how authors can add their own information to a section of music text: the lines that indicate the performers' portamentos were Robert Philip's, not Bach's. It is perfectly in order to apply markings or other graphics to a music extract to make a point. This may be especially helpful in writings about musical analysis. But care should be taken to ensure that this device is used to make your point clearer, not more obscure. These types of superimposition can clarify matters of musical analysis such as in the extract from Anna Butterworth's *Harmony in Practice* shown in Fig. 5.7.

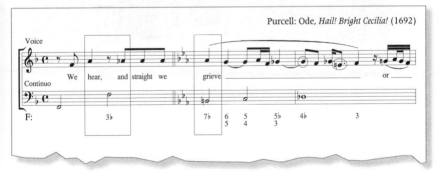

Fig. 5.7   This extract from Anna Butterworth's *Harmony in Practice* relates to an explanation given in its accompanying text. The boxes enable the author to identify sections on which she comments.

Paintings and other visual art

In captions for paintings, drawings and photographs (if they are to be used in detailed academic writing) the vital information to give is:
- the name of the artist or photographer;
- the title of the work;
- the date of the work.

Ideally, you should also say something about:
- the medium (for example, oil or watercolour);
- the size of the work;
- the gallery, collection or other location where the original is kept.

(The relevant citation procedures are explained in Chapter 11.)

Irrespective of the purpose of any pictorial illustration, it should be interesting, informative and capable of reproducing well. Fig. 5.8 (from the article 'Grand opéra' in *New Grove II*) is a good example of how an illustration is brought to life by the information contained in its caption.

2. The square at Altdorf, Act 3 scene ii of Rossini's 'Guillaume Tell': watercolour (probably by Franz Peirot) from a manuscript mise-en-scène (c1840) designed to convey details of the original Paris production of 1829 to provincial (and foreign) theatres intending to stage the opera

Fig. 5.8   An example of an informative caption that draws attention to the importance of the illustration.

Tables and lists

Tables (sometimes called charts) and lists (which are basically simple tables) are often used in writings about music. The way a table is laid out depends on the type of information it contains, but it must always be designed so that it is clear and easy to understand.

Tables contain information (or data) in columns (vertical lines) and rows (horizontal lines). Fig. 5.9, a reproduction of a table from Cyril Ehrlich's *The Piano: A History*, illustrates the growth of the piano manufacturing industry in England between 1870 and 1910. The notes explain the table and the way that the author has assembled the data.

Table X   The English Piano Industry: Total Output and Size of Enterprise 1870–1910

	Total Annual Production (in thousands of pianos)			Number of firms making			
	Claimed	Known firms	Serial Numbers	More than 2000	1000–2000	500–1000	300–500
	(1)	(2)	(3)	(4)	(5)	(6)	(7)
1870	20–25	23	10	2	1	3	10
1880	30–35	30	11	1	5	6	20
1890	50–90	30	12	0	10	9	21
1900	70–100	40	13	0	14	4	24
1910	75–100	50	22	5	18	3	24

Notes

Column 1 shows contemporary estimates. The low estimate for 1910 is in Dolge, op. cit., page 434.

Column 2 shows my own estimates, based on general information about known firms, in addition to serial number data. They are therefore probably under-estimates, excluding most shoddy and many 'stencilled' instruments.

Column 3 is based primarily upon production runs taken from reliable serial numbers. A few assessments have been added for those firms on which sufficient information is available to base a reasonable estimate of output. This column therefore represents an absolutely minimum estimate of total production.

The first Census of Production taken in 1907 provides an essential bench mark for these calculations. It gives output (UK) of pianos as 58,000 valued at £995,000. (Cd. 5545, ci 117, 1911. Census of Production, Part VII, Table I, page 46.)

Columns 4–7 are based on information about 840 firms drawn from music directories, trade journals, piano atlases and stock books.

Fig. 5.9   A reproduction of a table from Cyril Ehrlich's book *The Piano: A History*.

The table in Fig. 5.10 is more complex, with nineteen columns and forty-one rows. It shows 'the typical composition of orchestras for which works in the present-day repertory were originally written'. The columns have headings, and the explanatory note given at the

TABLE 1

Date	City	Institution	Violins	Violas	Cellos	Double Basses	Viols	Flutes	Oboes	Clarinets	Bassoons	Horns	Trumpets/Cornet(t)s	Trombones/Tubas	Timpani/other	Keyboard	Plucked strings	Repertory
1607	Mantua	Gonzaga Palace, theatre	4	4	2	2	3	2					4/2	4		6	6	Monteverdi *Orfeo*
1634	London	King's Violins, masque	4	7	4													William Lawes, Ives
1665	Venice	Teatro SS Giovanni e Paolo	2	2	1											3	2	Cavalli
1670s–80s	Paris	24 Violons du Roi, Opéra	6	12	6				2		2		1	2		1	1	Lully operas
1708	Rome	Palazzo Bonelli, oratorio	6	2	1	1										1		A. Scarlatti *Annunziata*
1708	Rome	Palazzo Bonelli, oratorio	23	4	6	6	1		4				2		1		1		Handel *La resurrezione*
1713	Venice	church	26	6	–12–											1	1	Caldara cantata
1728	London	King's Theatre	22	2	3	2			2		2		3		2	2	1	Handel operas
1730	Leipzig	Thomaskirche	6	4	2	1			3		2		3		1	2		Bach cantatas
1734	Dresden	court	12	4	5	2		3	3		2	2	2			2		Pisendel, Hasse, Vivaldi
1740s–50s	Naples	Teatro San Carlo	28	5	2	4			4		2	4				1	2	Porpora, Feo, Leo, Jommelli
1751	Paris	Opéra	16	6	7	5		2	3		4		1			1	1	Rameau
1754	London	Foundling Hospital Chapel	14	5	3	2			4		4					1		Handel *Messiah*
1754	Berlin	court	12	4	4	2	1	4	3		4	2	2		1	2	1	C.P.E. Bach, Graun, Quantz
1766	Venice	St Mark's church	12	6	4	5			2		2	2	2			2		Galuppi
1770s	Paris	Opéra	24	5	12	5		4	4	2	8	2	2			1	1	Gluck, Piccinni
1770s	Salzburg	court	18	2	2	1		1	2		3	2	2	3		1	1	Leopold and Wolfgang Mozart, Michael Haydn
1770s	Mannheim	court	20	4	4	4		3	3	3	4	2				1	1	Mannheim school, Stamitz, Mozart
1778	Paris	Concert Spirituel	22	6	9	6		2	2	2	2	2	2			1		Gossec, J.C. Bach, Mozart, Haydn, Paisiello
1782	Vienna		12	4	3	3		2	2		2	2	2			2		Mozart, Salieri etc
1783	Eszterháza	court	10	2	2	2			2			2	2					Haydn
1791–3	London	Hanover Square Rooms	16	4	4	4		2	2		2	2	2		1	1		Haydn
1813	Vienna	concert	8	2	2	2		2	2	2	2	2	2		1			Beethoven
1814	Vienna	Redoutensaal, concert	36	14	12	17		2	2	2	2	2	2	2	1			Beethoven
1814	Milan	Teatro alla Scala	25	6	4	8		2	2	2	2	4	2	1	1/1			Rossini
1818	Naples	Teatro San Carlo	24	6	6	7		2	2	2	2	4	2	3	1/1			Rossini
1824	Vienna	Kärntnertortheater, concert	24	10	6	6		2	2	2	2	2	2	2	1			Beethoven Ninth Symphony
1839	Leipzig	Gewandhaus, concert	17	5	5	4		2	2	2	2	2	2	2	1			Mendelssohn, Schumann
1839	Paris	Opéra	24	8	10	8		3	3	2	4	4	4	4	3		1/1	Meyerbeer, Halévy, Berlioz
1839	Paris	Opéra-Comique	16	5	6	6		3	3	3	6	3	4		?1		2	Auber, Boieldieu
1845	Turin	Teatro Regio	21	4	4	6		3	2	2	2	4	2	3		1	1	Donizetti, Verdi
1865	Leipzig	Gewandhaus, concert	30	8	9	5		2	2	2	2	4	2	3	1			Mendelssohn, Schumann etc
1876	Bayreuth	Festspielhaus	32	12	12	8		4	4	3	8	4	5	?/?			6	Wagner *Ring*
1867	Karlsruhe	court	18	4	4	4		2	2	2	3	4	2	3	1			Brahms First Symphony
1900	Vienna	Philharmonic Orchestra	33	11	10	10		4	4	4	4	8	4	5/1	2/3		1	Mahler, Strauss etc
1905	Turin	Teatro Regio	25	7	7	7		3	3	3	3	4	4	3/1	1/2		2	Puccini, Wagner
1929	Dresden	State Opera	33	11	11	11		6	6	6	6	10	6	6/1	2/4		1	Strauss
1934	London	Boyd Neel Orchestra, concert	11	3	3	2			2			2				1	1	Respighi, Holst, Elgar, Vaughan Williams
1974	New York	New York Philharmonic, concert	34	12	12	9		4	4	5	4	6	4	4/1	2/3	2	1	Boulez, Carter

Note: This chart attempts to show the typical composition of orchestras for which works in the present-day repertory were originally written. The figures have been drawn from standard reference works and from specialized studies listed in the bibliography. They must be taken as indicative in only a general sense, as forces varied from piece to piece, from occasion to occasion, and from year to year, as well as from place to place. To facilitate reference and comparison, instruments of the same families are grouped together without indication. Hence violins of all sizes appear in one column, as do: flutes, piccolos, alto flutes and recorders; oboes, english horns and tenor oboes; clarinets of all sizes; bassoons and double bassoons; trumpets and cornet(t)s; horns and Wagner tubas; and trombones of all sizes.

Fig. 5.10   A more complex table, devised by Neal Zaslaw, included in the entry 'Orchestra' in *The New Grove*.

foot of the table helps the reader to see the information in different ways – to compare parts of the table.

Transcribed text

Writers about music often need to quote the inscriptions on musical instruments or other texts (for example, title pages, or inscriptions on gravestones or monuments) in a way that shows the layout of the text as well as what it actually says. As shown in Fig. 5.11, this is done by:

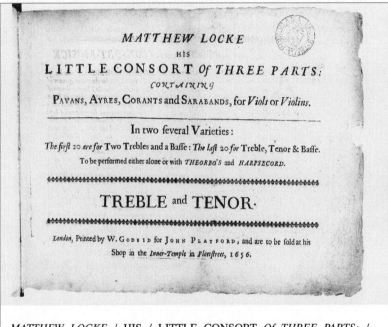

MATTHEW LOCKE / HIS / LITTLE CONSORT *Of THREE PARTS:* / CONTAINING / PAVANS, AYRES, CORANTS and SARABANDS, for *Viols* or *Violins.* / In two several Varieties: / *The first* 20 *are for* Two Trebles and a Basse: / *The last* 20 *for* Treble, Tenor & Basse. / To be performed either alone or with *THEORBO'S* and *HARPSECORD.* / TREBLE and TENOR. / *London*, Printed by W. GODBID for JOHN PLAYFORD, and are to be sold at his / Shop in the *Inner-Temple* in *Fleetstreet*, 1656.

Fig. 5.11   The title page of one of the partbooks of Matthew Locke's *Little Consort*. Below it the same information is given in transcription. This is based on Rosamond Harding's *A Thematic Catalogue of the Works of Matthew Locke.*

- treating the piece of text as you would a quotation: placing it in quotation marks and copying the lettering and punctuation exactly, with precise use of italics and upper and lower case letters;
- placing a slash mark (/) at the point of each line-break in the original.

Bibliography

Hoffmann, A., *Research for Writers*, 6th edn (London: A. & C. Black, 1999).

McCracken, R., and M. Gilbart, *Buying and Clearing Rights: Print, Broadcast and Multimedia* (London: Blueprint, 1995).

Writers' and Artists' Yearbook (London: A. & C. Black [published annually]), section on 'Copyright and libel'.

Part II

Chapter six

LANGUAGE AND NUMBERS

THIS CHAPTER is not a systematic guide to English language usage; it merely lists some of the most widely accepted conventions concerning the words, letters, numbers and punctuation that are frequently found in writings about music. Here, as throughout this book, the intention is not necessarily to suggest that there is only one way of doing things, but rather to provide examples that are legitimate and may be taken as the basis for consistency in your writing. I have concentrated on aspects of language and number usage that are often confused.

Abbreviations

(See also 'Latin abbreviations' below; Chapter 7, 'Arrangements, transcriptions and editions of music', 'Genres' and 'Performance directions'.)

Abbreviations abound in music writings as they do in other subjects, and they can be irritating when they are used too frequently. If you use an abbreviation you should explain its meaning the first time you use it. For example:

> One of the largest examining bodies is the London-based Associated Board of the Royal Schools of Music (ABRSM). It operates in several countries.

You can subsequently use the abbreviation ABRSM (usually left unpunctuated and without spaces between the letters: ABRSM, rather than A.B.R.S.M. or A B R S M).

As a general rule, a *contraction* – that is, an abbreviation that includes the first and last letters of the word in question – does not require a full stop (for instance, 'edn' for 'edition', or 'Mr' for 'Mister'). An abbreviation that does *not* include the last letter of the word *does* require a full stop (for instance, 'ed.' for 'editor', or 'Prof.'

for 'Professor'). However, sometimes musical abbreviations do not strictly follow this convention (see page 134).

If an abbreviation such as 'ed.', which takes a full stop, falls at the end of a sentence, you do not need to put in an extra full stop for the end of the sentence – one is sufficient.

Above, below

These two words are used to indicate a reference to something you have written or are about to write. If you wish to refer to something earlier in the page or on a previous page you might put, for example, 'For an illustration of flute keys see Chapter 2 above'. If you wish to refer to a later point in your writing you might put '... a fuller explanation of Handel's attitude to monarchy is given below'.

Acronyms

An acronym is formed by reducing a name or title to a set of initials that can be read as a word in its own right – for instance, *RILM*, pronounced 'rillum' (see Chapter 8, page 158). Italics are used for *RILM* simply because the letters stand for foreign words, *Répertoire international de littérature musicale* (see 'Foreign words' below); NATO (North Atlantic Treaty Organization), on the other hand, is not italicized. Acronyms are left unpunctuated and unspaced.

American and other spellings

Some words are spelled differently in American and UK English. Most word-processing programmes can be set to one mode of spelling or the other, and may also offer Australian, Canadian, Caribbean, New Zealand and South African English (amongst others). Determine whether you have to use one mode of spelling or another, and use it consistently. Remember to take account of variants in spelling when you use keywords for computer or on-line searches.

Apostrophe (')

The apostrophe is sometimes mistakenly used to indicate a plural form of a noun. For example:

There are two violin's in a string quartet.

This is wrong. The plural of *violin* is *violins* – without an apostrophe. Plurals are *never* formed with apostrophes.

The apostrophe has two main uses:

- It indicates that two words have been joined together, omitting some of the letters, as in:

He's singing (*He is* singing)
They aren't able to hear him (They *are not* able to hear him)

- It indicates possession:

The conductor's baton (The baton *of* the conductor)

But note that where a plural word is formed by adding 's' to the end (as it is in most cases in English), the apostrophe to indicate possession comes *after* the 's':

The conductors' batons (The batons of the conductors)

Take particular care with its/it's and whose/who's. In both these cases, the apostrophe indicates a *joining* of two words, *not* possession:

it + is = it's   who + is = who's

So:

It's raining.   Who's there?

but

The dog wagged its tail.   Whose hat is this?

Arabic numbering or numerals

This simply means the numbering most commonly used in Western countries: 1, 2, 3, 4...50, 51 and so on.

Brackets

ROUND BRACKETS OR PARENTHESES ( )

A round bracket is more properly called a 'parenthesis' (plural, parentheses). Parentheses must be used in pairs (an opening and a closing bracket). They indicate that the information contained within them is additional or incidental to the information conveyed in the rest of the sentence. For example:

He thought that the rock band played very badly (though it must be said that rock was not a style of music he had much time for).

Parentheses may also be used to enclose:
- certain types of references or parts of references (see Chapter 4, 'Short-title system' and 'Author–date system');
- a person's dates, or the date of a work or publication;
- alternative spellings of a word or name;
- foot- or endnote numbers (instead of superscript – see 'Subscript and superscript' below, and Chapter 4, 'How to cite sources in text: as footnotes, endnotes or in-text references?').

SQUARE BRACKETS [ ]
These are mainly used for inserting words into quotations (see 'Quotations' below). They are also used for a similar purpose when editing notated music.

ANGLE BRACKETS < >
These are used for enclosing e-mail and Web site addresses (see Chapter 11, 'Internet sources'). They are never themselves part of the address – that is, you never type them with the address when you want to send an e-mail or search for a Web site. Their purpose is to mark off the address from any text that surrounds it. In particular, there is a danger of confusion between the dots that form an essential part of an electronic address and ordinary punctuation marks, especially full stops. Placing the address in angle brackets solves this problem by separating any punctuation mark from the last character of the address:

The author can be contacted at <r.v.williams@symph.com>.

The address is *only* the characters between the two angle brackets.

-ce and -se

In UK usage, the *-ce* ending indicates a noun, and the *-se* ending indicates a verb. For example:

Noun	Verb
the practice	to practise
the licence	to license
the advice	to advise

(In American usage, however, 'practise' and 'license' are the spellings for both the noun and the verb.)

Centuries

You should normally refer to centuries in words rather than figures – for instance, 'the eighteenth century' rather than 'the 18th century' or 'the 18th C'. When used as a compound adjective (see 'Joined or compound words' below), the two words should be hyphenated:

an eighteenth-century composer

But they should not be hyphenated for:

Beethoven was born in the eighteenth century

Clichés

A cliché is an expression that has become overused, and as a result has lost much of its original force and sharpness. For instance, phrases such as 'at the end of the day', 'from bitter experience' and 'the bottom line' are clichés. While clichés have a place in spoken language and some forms of writing (such as journalism or fiction), they are best avoided in academic writing.

Commas and full stops (periods)

These punctuation marks are the most crucial to the clarity of sentences. Making sure that a sentence is properly punctuated, and, in particular, understanding the difference between a comma and a full stop (also called a period), can be the key to writing clearer, better-structured sentences. A sentence must always end with a full stop, or with a question mark if it is a question, or an exclamation mark if it is a command or exclamation. Apart from its use in some abbreviations (see above), this is the main use of the full stop.

The most common mistake with commas is to use one after a group of words that is in fact a sentence, and should thus be concluded with a full stop. A comma indicates a brief pause within a sentence, not the end of a sentence. Don't overuse commas – the pause a comma creates should help the reader to understand what you mean, not break the sentence up so much that it becomes irritating and disjointed. However, commas are important, and can make a fundamental difference to the meaning of a sentence. For example:

Anna, the soloist has just arrived.

In this instance, the sentence seems to be addressed to a person called Anna, telling her that the soloist has just arrived. But if a further comma is added, the sense is quite different:

Anna, the soloist, has just arrived.

Now it means that the soloist, who is called Anna, has just arrived.

The following are examples of the main uses of commas:
- A pair of commas can perform the same function as round brackets or parentheses (see pages 95–6), marking off information that is additional or incidental to the main message of the sentence:

  The soloist, whose name was Anna Martin, was young and not well known.

- A comma marks off a word or phrase such as 'However' or 'Of course', which makes a link between two sentences:

  She has a fine voice. However, she is very inexperienced.

- A *pair* of commas is used to mark off a word or phrase such as 'however' or 'of course' when it occurs in the middle of a sentence:

  He did not, however, play the piece very expressively.

- Commas are used to separate a group of adjectives in a sentence:

  The song was tedious, sentimental, embarrassing and badly sung.

- They are also used to separate the items in a list:

  The band is made up of a drummer, a lead guitarist, a bass guitarist, a keyboard player and a singer.

  While it is usual *not* to put a comma before the final 'and' in UK usage, it is not technically wrong to do so, and indeed it is common practice in some publishing houses and in American English.

Compound words

See 'Joined or compound words' below.

Countries, towns and nationalities

(See also 'He/she and other forms of bias' below.)

The names and boundaries of countries have changed over the centuries. Italy and Germany are examples of countries that have become unified only relatively recently, and which for much of their modern history have comprised numerous smaller states. Thus it is likely to be more accurate to define fifteenth-century 'Italian' composers, for example, by the state from which they came or in which they worked – a fifteenth-century *Florentine* composer, for instance.

It is important to be historically accurate and to avoid anachronisms. Take care, for example, in referring to the area now covered by the Netherlands and Belgium. The Netherlands formerly included Belgium but does so no longer, and the area was often referred to as 'the Low Countries'. The names 'Holland' and 'the Netherlands' are not interchangeable – Holland covers only part of the modern Netherlands.

The names of towns and cities may need special thought. They too have sometimes been changed, as with Leningrad, which reverted to its earlier name of St Petersburg following the break-up of the Soviet Union; and Salisbury (Rhodesia), which became Harare when Rhodesia gained independence and took the name Zimbabwe. There are other special considerations: several towns in Northern Europe are called Freiburg or Fribourg, just as many states in the USA have towns called Springfield, for instance. This means that it is often necessary to qualify the name of a town or city with the name of the state or region in which it is found. In writings in the English language, the names of towns and cities can properly be given in their English spelling, as with Nuremberg (Nürnberg in German), and Milan (Milano in Italian).

The terms 'American' and 'English' should also be used carefully. Canadians are Canadians, not Americans; and Scots, Welsh and Northern Irish are British but not English, while the people of Eire (the Republic of Ireland) are referred to as Irish. On the same note, New Zealanders are not Australians.

The best way to determine a musician's nationality or birthplace is to look at the relevant entry in *New Grove II*. Or, if a contemporary musician does not have a *Grove* entry, you might see whether there is an official Web site that carries his or her biography.

Cyrillic lettering

The Cyrillic script is the alphabet of languages such as Russian that have a Slavonic origin (Fig. 6.1). Word-processing packages and type-faces that are designed for European languages with a different origin, such as English or French, do not usually accommodate these letters, and so Russian and other Slavonic words are generally transliterated (see 'Transliteration' below).

Fig. 6.1
Cyrillic title
page of
collected piano
works by
Tchaikovsky.

П. ЧАЙКОВСКИЙ.

СОБРАНИЕ СОЧИНЕНИЙ

для фортепиано

Dated language (how to avoid it)

Your writing will become inaccurate and begin to look dated very quickly if you use terms like 'last year', 'three years ago', 'in the last few years', 'at the moment' and so on. It is better to get into the habit of referring to the precise year, or to the decade or part of the century ('in the 1990s', 'in the early twenty-first century' and so on).

Dates

(See also 'Centuries' above and 'Decades' below.)

In British usage, 12.4.00 means 12 April 2000; but in the USA, it can mean 4 December 2000. So to avoid confusion, while days and years should be given as figures, months are best given as words:

July 1997
26 March 2000

It is acceptable, but not necessary, to place a comma between the month and year:

26 March, 2000

When a range of years is given, it is usually abbreviated:

1956–8   (UK usage)
1956–58   (USA usage)

But in both UK and USA usage, with the numbers 11 to 19, use:

1810–11 *not* 1810–1

because the final number is spoken as 'eleven', not 'one'. Similarly, use:

1716–18 *not* 1716–8

because the final number is spoken as 'eighteen', not 'eight'.

The phrases *Anno Domini* ('In the Year of the Lord', AD) and 'Before Christ' (BC) are now often replaced by 'Common Era' (CE) and 'Before the Common Era' (BCE) respectively.

Decades

These should not contain apostrophes:

1880s, *not* 1880's
the fifties, *not* the 'fifties *or* the '50s

Diacritics and special characters

Diacritics are marks such as accents and dots that appear above or below letters, influencing the sound or meaning of a word.

These are examples of diacritics:

Ö ā î Š è á ç ů Ṛ

Special characters are letters that do not occur in the typeface normally used by a typesetter. For example, the usual English typeface would not include the German ß (Eszett), which represents double 's'.

It is important to use diacritics or special characters accurately; a letter with an accent has a different sound from the same letter without one. Word-processing programmes do not contain all the diacritics that one might encounter. For example, few have the Welsh ŷ. It is important to mark diacritics by hand if they cannot be word-processed.

Ellipsis (pl. ellipses) (...)

You use an ellipsis – that is, three dots – to show that you have omitted part of a quotation. This is described in more detail under 'Quotations' below.

Figures of speech and colloquialisms

This refers to phrases used in ordinary spoken language and the appropriateness of their use in written text. The problem is a tricky one: some such phrases have no place at all in certain types of writing, though they make other forms of writing more lively and enjoyable. In some areas – jazz, for example – the specialist terms are often drawn from figures of speech and colloquialisms.

Here are some broad guidelines.

- Do not use figures of speech unless you really need to or intend to; don't allow figures of speech to be part of your ordinary language in academic writing.
- Use scare quotes (see 'Quotation marks' below) to bring attention to the fact that you are using a figure of speech:

The horn player (who had miscounted his bars' rest) 'dropped a clanger' by playing his solo a bar early.

But even here you will see that the colloquialism adds little to the meaning of the phrase.

Foreign words

If you need to write a word that comes from a language other than English, it should be written in italics, with the appropriate diacritics (see above) if there are any. (But see also 'Foreign words that have been anglicized' below, and Chapter 7, 'Performance directions'.)

Foreign words that have been anglicized

Some words from languages other than English have become so thoroughly assimilated into ordinary English use that they no longer need to be treated as foreign. When a non-English word has such a status it is usually unnecessary for it to be given in italics. It is also acceptable for any accent that the word might have in its original language to be

omitted, as long as this does not make the pronunciation unclear.
Here is a selection of anglicized words:

cliché (French)	Frau/Herr (German)
concerto (Italian)	Madame/Monsieur (Fr.)
conservatoire (Fr.)	premiere (Fr.)
debut (Fr.)	protégé (Fr.)
elite (Fr.)	repertoire (Fr.)
fiancé (Fr.)	Señor/Señora (Sp.)
flamenco (Spanish)	Signor/Signora (It.)
franc (Fr.)	virtuoso (It.)

Words of Italian origin such as 'concerto', 'libretto' and 'virtuoso'
become 'concerti', 'libretti' and 'virtuosi' in the Italian plural, but it is
also generally acceptable (and, some would argue, less fussy) to form
an English plural by simply adding an 's' – 'virtuosos', 'librettos' and
'concertos' (see also Chapter 7, 'Genres').

Full stops

See 'Commas and full stops' above.

He/she and other forms of bias (how to avoid them)

Avoid bias in the language you use. In other words, do not give the
impression that your writing either deliberately excludes or inadver-
tently overlooks people whose background and experience is different
from your own. The most familiar example of bias in language is the
routine use of the male pronouns (he/him/his), or the nouns 'man' or
'mankind', in contexts where the person or people in question could
just as well be female; but you should also be sensitive to other
possible issues such as race or nationality.

Mere 'political correctness' is simply irritating, and will distract
attention from your argument. It is best to use neutral and inclusive
language in the least obtrusive way possible. For instance, the use of
's/he' is rather awkward and unsatisfactory, and repeated use of 'he or
she' is not much of an improvement, though either of these methods
may be used. It is much better to rephrase the sentence altogether, so
as to use the pronouns 'one', 'we', 'you' or 'they'.

The following sentence is an example of gender bias:

> When a person first performs a solo, his greatest obstacle is lack of confidence.

There is no reason for the person mentioned here to be a man. To avoid the problem, the sentence could be reworded in a number of ways:

> When one first performs a solo, one's greatest obstacle is lack of confidence.

Or less formally:

> When you first perform a solo, your greatest obstacle is lack of confidence.

Or a yet different pronoun:

> When we first perform a solo, our greatest obstacle is lack of confidence.

Or you could avoid mentioning a person altogether (this is possibly the best formulation – it is certainly the most concise):

> The greatest obstacle in solo performance is lack of confidence.

In certain historical or cultural contexts, however, it may be a matter of simple accuracy to use a specific gender pronoun. You might, for instance, be discussing military bands in a period or society in which they always consisted of men only.

Don't assume that bias only arises where offence is caused; you are also being biased if you put your reader at a disadvantage in some way – for instance, by failing to explain for the benefit of readers from another country the meaning of an abbreviation which you take for granted.

Bias of any description also makes your ideas seem narrow and parochial. One form of bias is the use of a phrase such as 'in this country'. This looks innocent, but makes the sweeping assumption that all your readers are from the same national and cultural background as you yourself. If you need to make an observation about a national characteristic or practice, then specify the country in question by name, even if it is your own country of origin.

Hyphens

See 'Joined or compound words' and 'Numbers' below and 'Centuries' above.

-ise and -ize

Where *-ise* or *-ize* is added to a word to make a verb (e.g., civil – to civilise/civilize; character – to characterise/characterize), American English uses a 'z' spelling. UK usage often accepts either spelling, but there are exceptions where only the 's' spelling can be used. One such exception is for certain verbs that are related to a noun which is already spelled with an -is- (e.g., the advert*is*ement – to advert*ise*). Thus it follows that there are a number of verbs that can only be spelled with *–ise*, never with *–ize*. You should check in a dictionary if you are unsure.

Italics

Italics are used to make a particular element stand out from the text around it. One major use is for titles of works. Several kinds of titles should be given in italics:
• published books;
• journals and periodicals (but not the articles they contain);
• musical works given descriptive titles by the composer (see Chapter 10, 'Music compositions');
• paintings, photographs and sculptures;
• plays, films, and radio and television programmes;
• long poems (i.e., poems that are to all intents and purposes books in themselves).

Other kinds of title are dealt with in 'Quotation marks' below. (See also Chapter 9, 'Religious writings'.)

Italics are also used for foreign words (see above) and to emphasize a particular word or phrase (though this use should be applied sparingly, or the effect can be distracting and irritating). Italics are also sometimes used for sub-headings.

Be careful with punctuation when using italics. Any punctuation marks that fall *within* an italic phrase or title should also be in italics.

However, punctuation that *follows* an italic phrase or title, but is not an intrinsic part of it, should be put back into roman. For example:

> A useful work on the subject is Ehrlich's *Harmonious Alliance: A History of the Performing Right Society*, published to coincide with the PRS's 75th anniversary.

Here, the colon, which forms part of the title, is in italics, but the comma, which does not, is in roman.

Joined or compound words

Terms that are made up of more than one word – that is, compound words – are often joined by a hyphen (-), particularly where the sense would otherwise be confusing. A hyphen indicates that the two or more parts it connects do not have the required meaning when taken separately.

A term such as 'barrel organ', which is made up of two nouns, may be hyphenated for the sake of clarity ('barrel-organ'), but since there is little possibility of confusion here, the hyphen is not necessary. American style uses fewer hyphens than British, but in British style also there is an increasing trend towards less frequent use of hyphenation, particularly in compound nouns. Older or more conservative dictionaries will often hyphenate such words where more recent dictionaries do not. The best advice is to check in a recent dictionary, or use a hyphen if you think confusion might arise without it.

Another kind of compound term is the compound adjective, and here it is almost always necessary to use a hyphen. For example, while it is clear that 'a light-blue bag' refers to the colour of the bag, 'a light blue bag' appears also to refer to its weight. Similarly, while the phrase 'his best-known works' clearly means 'his most famous works', written without a hyphen 'his best known works' means 'the best of his known works'.

Sometimes it is necessary to use a hyphen after a prefix. Prefixes such as 're-' and 'un-' are often attached directly on to a word – for instance, 'rescoring'. However, you would have to think twice about the meaning of 'reenter', whereas 're-enter' is immediately clear. It is worth remembering that a hyphen is necessary if the word following the prefix begins with a capital letter – for instance, 'post-Renaissance'. You should use a hyphen where the pronunciation and sense of the word might otherwise be unclear.

Latin abbreviations

In the main body of your writing it is best to use the full English word or phrase if possible. For instance, it is good practice to avoid abbreviations such as 'e.g.' and 'i.e.' altogether, and to use the phrases 'for example' and 'that is' instead. However, you may want to use such abbreviations in foot- or endnotes, where you should be as brief and economical as possible.

The following list contains the most common Latin abbreviations. Some (generally the most commonly used) are put in roman, while others are still treated as foreign words and put in italics. Note the use of full stops:

c., *ca*	*circa*; about. Used with approximate dates (*c.*1900 or *ca*1900, meaning 'around 1900'). Use one form or the other consistently.
cf.	*confer*; compare. This should not be used except in foot- or endnotes.
eadem	*the same.* Its function is to avoid repeating a female author's name in successive references, but it is no longer widely used and is best avoided. (See also *idem.*)
e.g.	*exempli gratia*; for example. The full English phrase is better than the abbreviation.
et al.	*et alii*; and other (people). Restrict use to shortened note or in-text references to works with more than two authors (Jones *et al.*). (However, *et al.* is also the abbreviation for *et alibi*, meaning 'and elsewhere'.)
etc.	*et cetera*; and so on. Again, try to express this without using the abbreviation.
fl	*floruit*; flourished. Used to indicate the period when a person is known to have been active if birth and death dates are not known (*fl* 1573–1601).
ibid.	*ibidem*; in the same place. Used in notes to refer again to the same page of a book that was referred to in the note *immediately before* (or to the same book, but a different page, in which case *ibid.* must be followed by the page number).
idem	*the same.* Its function is to avoid repeating a male author's name in successive references, but it is no longer widely used and is best avoided. (See also *eadem.*)

i.e.   *id est*; that is. The English phrase is preferred to the abbreviation.

loc. cit.   *loco citato*; in the passage cited. Used with the author's name to indicate the same work and page as in a recent reference. This is another phrase that is generally avoided.

op. cit.   *opere citato*; in the work cited. Used with the author's name to indicate the same work as in a recent reference. This is another one to avoid if you can.

s.v.   *sub verbo*; under the word (or, see under). Used for references to dictionary and encyclopedia entries (for instance, 'This is described in *Grove*, s.v. "Tom-tom".', meaning the *Grove* entry on 'tom-tom').

viz.   *videlicet*; namely ('The horn players, viz. Schmidt and Nagel, were reappointed a year later.'). The English word is preferable.

Lower case and upper case

Lower case and upper case are the phrases used to describe (respectively) non-capital (small) letters and capital letters:

this is lower case
THIS IS UPPER CASE

Money

Amounts of money follow the same basic rules for all numbers (see 'Numbers' below). Exact amounts should be written in figures, except where they are so large as to look awkward. (Millions, for example, are usually best given as a combination of figure and word: $3 million.)

The same pattern is used for most currencies. That is, if you are referring to several amounts of money, some of which are whole pounds or dollars, for example, and others of which are (or include) pennies or cents, you should express them all using the pound sign (£) or dollar sign ($), rather than mix pounds and pence, dollars and cents:

The manuscript book cost £8.00, the notebook cost £1.75 and the pen cost £0.49.

not:

> The manuscript book cost £8, the notebook cost £1.75 and the pen cost 49p.

There is no need to italicize currency symbols and abbreviations such as $ (dollar), ¢ (cent), £ (pound) and DM (Deutschmark), or put full stops after abbreviations such as p (penny) or F (franc).

Some countries share the name of a currency. If you need to distinguish between different currencies with the same name, you should indicate the country in question by putting the initial letter or abbreviation of the country before the dollar sign. For instance:

A$750.00 (Australia)	C$25.00 (Canada)	US$3.50 (USA)
NZ$17.75 (New Zealand)	HK$300.00 (Hong Kong)	
BFr450.00 (Belgium)	SFr1150.00 (Switzerland)	
FFr62.40 (France)		

If you deal with historical topics, you will encounter old-style currencies (for example, in publishers' and instrument makers' catalogues). Similar rules apply to old currencies. (For an explanation of how to find information about old currencies, see Mitchell, *International Historical Statistics*, cited in the bibliography at the end of Chapter 8.)

Numbers

(See also 'Centuries', 'Dates', 'Decades', 'Money', 'Page and folio references' and 'Roman numbering or numerals'.)

The question with numbers is whether to spell them out in words or to use figures. Two basic rules of thumb are that small or approximate numbers should be written in words, while large or exact ones should be in figures. On this basis:

- All numbers lower than 100 should usually be written as words – 'one', 'two', 'fifty-five', 'seventy-two' and so on, except for precise quantities and measurements, percentages and cross-references (for example, to a page or chapter number).
- Anything higher should generally be given in figures – 159, 2,350 etc., except where it is clearer and neater to use words (for example, 'two million', as opposed to 2,000,000).
- In arts and humanities writing, numbers of a thousand and upwards are usually written with a comma in front of the last

three digits (for example, 2,000). Omitting the comma is more typical of mathematical or scientific practice. (Numbers of a million and upwards include a comma in front of the last three digits and each further group of three digits – for example, 5,000,000.)

- If a number forms the first word of a sentence, it should be written as a word, not as a figure.

When written as words, numbers such as those between twenty-one and twenty-nine, thirty-one and thirty-nine and so on should be hyphenated:

He had forty-four pianos and sixty-eight harpsichords in his collection.

Page and folio references

This is an important, if slightly complicated, matter, and there is no option but to explain it in detail. A single sheet of paper in a book or manuscript is called a leaf. Usually, the leaves of a book are called pages, and the numbering of the leaves is called pagination. However, in some works (such as music manuscripts and other historical manuscripts), the leaves are sometimes called folios rather than pages, and the numbering is called foliation. The main practical distinction between a page and a folio is that the word 'page' refers to just one side of a leaf (so if the front of the leaf is page 1, the back will be page 2), whereas the word 'folio' refers to the *whole* leaf, both front and back (so *both* sides of the leaf constitute folio 1). Manuscripts, including music manuscripts, are often referred to as a collection of folios.

In references to works that are paginated, the abbreviation 'p.' for 'page' is used, and the plural, 'pages', is given as 'pp.'. You may come across a reference such as 'pp. 78f.', the 'f.' meaning 'following page'; this indicates that you should look at page 78 and page 79. A reference such as 'pp. 78ff.' indicates that you should look at page 78 and an unspecified number of following pages. It is preferable to avoid this lack of clarity in your writing and give precise page numbers, such as 'pp. 78–9' or 'pp. 78–82'.

In references to works that are foliated, various abbreviations are possible. Some people use 'f.' (folio) and 'ff.' (folios), but this risks confusion with the abbreviations for 'following page' and 'following pages' that I mentioned above. The usual American version is 'fol.' (folio) and 'fols.' (folios), while British publishers favour 'fo.' (folio) and 'fos.' (folios). Thus a reference to folio 42 of a manuscript would be given as:

fo. 42

and a reference to folios 17 to 23 would be given as:

fos. 17–23

Even though 'folio' refers to both sides of the leaf, there needs to be a way of distinguishing between one side and the other, because the writer or composer may well have written on both sides of the folio. In this case the front of the leaf (or the right-hand page, if the folios are sewn into a book) is referred to as the recto, for which the abbreviation 'r.' is used. The back of the leaf (or the left-hand page in a book) is called the verso, for which the abbreviation 'v.' is used. So a single side of a folio could be referred to like this:

fo. 42r.

If it is a long passage which starts on the verso (back) of fo. 17, and finishes on the recto (front) of fo. 23, the reference will be:

fos. 17v.–23r.

Plurals of words originating in Latin or Greek

The English language contains numerous words that originate in Latin or Greek. They frequently cause difficulty for two reasons. First, it is easy to confuse the singular and the plural form. 'Criteria' and 'phenomena' (both plurals) are often used where 'criterion' and 'phenomenon' (singular) are intended, for example. Secondly, the plural does not follow the common English practice of simply adding an 's'. If in doubt, you should check them in a dictionary, but here is a selection of such words, in both their singular and plural forms:

Singular	Plural
appendix	appendices
crisis	crises
criterion	criteria
curriculum	curricula

datum	data
ellipsis	ellipses (see 'Ellipsis' above and 'Quotations' below)
erratum	errata
formula	formulae
hypothesis	hypotheses
index	indices (though 'indexes' is also correct)
medium	media
memorandum	memoranda
parenthesis	parentheses (see 'Brackets' above)
phenomenon	phenomena
sigillum	sigla (see Chapter 11)
stimulus	stimuli
stratum	strata
thesis	theses

Pronouns

Pronouns are words that take the place of nouns – for instance, the noun 'the woman' might be replaced by the pronouns 'she' or 'her'. It is essential to be consistent in the use of pronouns. Here is some general advice:

- The pronoun you adopt should be appropriate for the style and purpose of your writing.
- In academic writing you should generally avoid personal pronouns (I, you, we and so on), unless, for example, you are specifically required to give your own judgement or view, and thus to introduce a more personal element into your writing. 'One' is a useful pronoun for academic writing, because of its more general and impersonal tone. (In this book, however, because it is a didactic (teaching) text, I deliberately chose to use the pronouns 'I' and 'you'.)

Quotation marks (quotes)

In UK usage, single quotation marks or quotes (' ') are used more often than double quotes (" "). Double quotes are used in UK publications mainly to enclose passages of dialogue in fictional works, and where it is necessary to use a second set of quotation marks within the first set (see Fig. 6.2, point (6) on page 115). In the USA, however, double quotes are generally preferred.

Quotes are used in the following circumstances:

- When you need to draw attention to a word – for instance, if it has a specialized meaning or doesn't quite mean what it normally means, as in:

The trumpeter 'bent' the first note of each phrase.

- When you need to give the meaning of a word, as in:

'Quotes' is another term for 'quotation marks'.

- When you need to identify a quotation of someone else's words, as in:

Williams calls him 'the most brilliant player of his generation'.

- When you want to use scare quotes (sometimes called sneer quotes) to distance yourself from a term or idea (see also 'Figures of speech and colloquialisms' above). For instance, you may wish your reader to understand that you are being ironic or don't subscribe to the idea yourself, as in:

The idea of his 'brilliance' as a player has, it seems, gone unquestioned.

- When you are giving the titles of certain kinds of works – primarily individual songs, short poems, journal and newspaper articles, and chapters in books. (See 'Italics' above for other kinds of title.)

Quotations

(See also 'Quotation marks' above.)

Quotations from the work of other writers should be used sparingly, unless you are writing about another person's writings. It is generally best to express what you want to say in your own words, as this will make you think more carefully about what you really mean, and will demonstrate that you have fully understood the sources you have read. However, it is useful to quote from another writer when:

- you wish to draw attention to the writer's exact words (for example, in order to show that he or she really did say something in a particular way);

- you wish to cite the evidence on which you have based a particular point;
- you feel that the writer has expressed a particular point or idea especially memorably or effectively.

Short quotations (that is, quotations of less than about three lines) should continue as part of the sentence in the main text, but should be enclosed in quotation marks, as in Fig. 6.2, point (1). Quotations longer than about three lines should be 'displayed'. That is, they should be separated from the main text by missing a line above and below the quotation, and indenting the whole quotation so that there is an obvious difference between the left-hand margin of the main text and that of the quoted text, as in Fig. 6.2, point (3). (Some publishers also set indented quotations in a different font size.)

You may find that it is necessary to edit a quotation in some way so as to clarify it or fit it grammatically into the rest of your sentence (though you must be careful that your alterations do not distort the original meaning of the words). You may need to insert or omit a word or words. If you insert words into a quotation, they should be enclosed within square brackets, as in Fig. 6.2, point (4). This shows that the words are yours and are not in the original writer's text.

If you omit part of the text, you should indicate this with an ellipsis – that is, a row of three dots (…), as in Fig. 6.2, point (5). The omission of one or more paragraphs should be indicated by an ellipsis at the end of the paragraph preceding the omission. If an ellipsis falls immediately before a full stop, you may use a fourth dot to indicate the full stop, but this is not necessary. It is also usually unnecessary to use an ellipsis at the beginning or end of a quotation, even if the sentence is incomplete. Say, for example, that you wanted to quote from the *Grove* entry on Scott Joplin:

> Joplin, born in Texas in the 1860s, was often said to have '…had few early educational opportunities…'.

To use ellipses in this way is correct, but superfluous. They indicate that 'had' is not the start of the sentence from which the words are quoted, while 'opportunities' is not the end of the sentence. But since it is in the nature of any quotation to be merely an extract, there is no need to announce the fact so scrupulously. Thus the following is perfectly acceptable and, indeed, less fussy:

any sort of approach. It therefore follows that Barnes may well have been correct when he said that the early music revival was "certainly *a movement* [my italics] but a movement of noble intent that turned into a fetish" He, like Martin and others who were at the heart of the revival in the 1960s, noticed a growing obsession with what was musically unusual, cute and quaint. Indeed, Martin became an outspoken critic of the use of the term 'authentic performance', a term he decried in his famous 1971 radio interview with Marcus O'Neill. He told O'Neill that audiences were being duped into a belief that they were experiencing an accurate reproduction of the past:

Who on earth thinks that musical authenticity is really possible? There are so many gaps in our knowledge. In any case, are we to believe that musicians leave their cultural baggage in the dressing room when they go on stage to perform Josquin or Lassus? Are we to believe that [London] audiences turn medieval when they cross to the South Bank, [and] enter a world where modern life and its accumulated impact is erased? Do people not see that even the best performance of, say, sixteenth-century music, is little more than a sort of musical experiment?[6]

Writing more than a decade later, in 1985, Martin was no more sanguine about the state of early music performance, complaining that 'compact discs with titles like "The Renaissance Hit Parade" are pedalled [sic] by musicians with an entirely straight face'.[7] This was shortly after he acrimoniously severed his ten-year relationship with Corpus Magnus Records.

Martin's views are not, of course, universally held. Others see the popularising of earlier repertoires and practices as a means through which audiences

Fig. 6.2   **Quotations**

1 Short quotation, enclosed in quotes.
2 Use of [my italics] to identify an emphasis that was not in the original text.
3 Long, displayed quotation.
4 Use of square brackets to identify words introduced into text to clarify the meaning.
5 Use of ellipsis to identify words omitted from the text because they are unnecessary for the purposes of the quotation.
6 Use of double quotes within single quotes.
7 Use of [*sic*] to indicate a misspelling ('pedalled' for 'peddled') in the original text.

Joplin, born in Texas in the 1860s, was often said to have 'had few early educational opportunities'.

If, however, you are concerned that the sense of the original may be altered by your selection of only certain words from it, you should put an ellipsis (or ellipses if necessary) in place of the omitted words, to show that the writer said more on the point in question than you have chosen to quote.

If you wish to draw attention to a particular word or words within a quotation, you should italicize them as you would for emphasis in your own text, but after the italicized word or words you should then put in square brackets the words '[my italics]', as in Fig. 6.2, point (2).

You should always quote accurately, giving the exact punctuation and spelling used in your source. If it contains a typographical error, a misspelling or an old-fashioned spelling, you should not amend it; instead you should put the word '*sic*' (Latin for 'so' or 'in this way') in italics and square brackets after the word, to show that it is spelled in this way in the original (see Fig. 6.2, point (7)).

Recto and verso

See 'Page and folio references' above.

Roman lettering

In this sense, the word 'roman' is used to describe letters that are not in italics (see above). So:

This is in italics
This is in roman

Roman numbering or numerals

In Western countries this is the alternative to arabic numbering. Roman numbering uses letters rather than figures. They may be given as capital or lower-case letters – that is, the arabic '1' may be expressed as 'I' or 'i' in roman numbers. Roman numbering is less widely used than arabic, but its use is common all the same – for one thing, it is of course used to describe chords (I–ii–V^7–I, for example). Sometimes years are given in roman numbers – for example, at the end of a television programme or film, you may see the year in which it was made expressed as a roman number. The basic roman numbers are as follows:

I (= 1)	II (= 2)	III (= 3)	IV (= 4)	V (= 5)
VI (= 6)	VII (= 7)	VIII (= 8)	IX (= 9)	X (= 10)
XX (= 20)	XXX (= 30)	XL (= 40)	L (= 50)	LX (= 60)
LXX (= 70)	LXXX (= 80)	XC (= 90)	C (= 100)	D (= 500)
M (= 1000)				

All other numbers are combinations of these. For example:

23 = XXIII	49 = XLIX	78 = LXXVIII	99 = XCIX

Running heads

A running head is the shortened version of a title that is often placed at the top of each page of a published book or article. These running heads are always inserted by the publisher rather than by the author.

Sentences

As I said earlier, this chapter is not intended to be a systematic or comprehensive grammar guide, but it is worth looking briefly at one of the most basic aspects of written English. Many people have trouble recognizing what is and what is not a complete sentence. This is hardly surprising, because the sentence is one of those things that we tend to assume we understand, when it is really quite difficult to define simply and succinctly. In fact, rather than trying to define what a sentence is, it is better to think about what a sentence must *contain* in order to be a sentence. Difficulty with writing proper sentences often comes down to a problem with punctuation rather than with sentence structure in its own right, so you should also look at 'Commas and full stops' above, but it is helpful to understand the basic elements that make up a sentence.

THE BASIC ELEMENTS OF A SENTENCE

All sentences must contain a verb. A verb is a word that expresses an action or a condition: 'to play', 'to sing', 'to seem', 'to feel' and so on.

A sentence must also contain a subject of that verb (that is, a pronoun such as 'I' or 'they', or a noun such as 'John' or 'the singer', for example).

If you are unsure what the subject of the verb is, take the sentence:

She played the violin.

The verb is 'played', because 'played' is the action that took place. To find the subject, ask yourself who or what played. There are only two possibilities – 'She' or 'the violin'. The violin is the thing that was played, not the thing that did the playing so it is the object of the verb. 'She' is the one who played so the subject of the verb is 'she'.

It is not always necessary for a sentence to have an object. You could take away the words 'the violin', and you would still have a sentence:

She played.

This makes sense in its own right.

If you take away the subject 'She', however, leaving the words 'played the violin' you are left with just the verb and the object, and these alone do not really make sense. They leave us wondering *who* played the violin. So you cannot have a sentence without a verb and its subject. A more compact way of saying 'a verb and its subject' is the term 'a finite verb'.

CLAUSES

A sentence is made up of one or more clauses. A clause is a group of words that contains a finite verb. The following are all clauses:

He sang
He sang badly
He sang the tenor solo

The key point is that each example contains the finite verb 'he sang' – that is, the verb 'sang', together with its subject, 'he'.

There are two basic kinds of clause – a *main clause* and a *subordinate clause*. A main clause makes sense in its own right. It can work as a sentence with nothing further added to it. The three examples given above are main clauses and also simple sentences. (A simple sentence is one that is made up of just one main clause.)

However, a *subordinate clause* does not make sense in its own right. It adds information to a main clause, and cannot stand as a sentence on its own: it is literally subordinate, or secondary, to the main clause (though this does not mean that it has to *follow* the main clause – subordinate clauses often make just as much sense *before* main clauses).

Take the sentence:

He sang the tenor solo badly because he did not know it well enough.

The main clause is 'He sang the tenor solo badly'. This could form a sentence in its own right. However, the clause 'because he did not know it well enough' could not; it seems to beg the question 'what didn't he know well enough?' or 'what couldn't he do?'. More information needs to be added to it in order to make a complete sentence. So 'because he did not know it well enough' is a subordinate clause. Subordinate clauses should not be written as sentences in their own right, but should always be attached to a main clause.

As a rule of thumb, be careful when you use words such as 'because', 'although', 'though', 'despite', 'whereas' and 'while', as these often signal a subordinate clause. Check that you have written a complete sentence, and have not left a subordinate clause begging further information.

Subscript and superscript

Subscript is a small letter, number or symbol placed *below* a full-sized letter or number. For example, sharp and flat signs are sometimes printed in subscript – for example, C♯. (See Chapter 7, 'Keys'.)

Superscript is a small letter, number or symbol placed *above* a full-sized letter or number, for example, as a foot- or endnote number (see Chapter 4, 'How to cite sources in text: as footnotes, endnotes or in-text references?'). For instance, let's assume that the following quotation will lead to the ninth foot- or endnote in your essay:

The Sixties have been called 'the cultural revolution of the twentieth century',[9] particularly for pop music.

As you can see, the superscript '9' is placed at the end of the quotation, *after* the closing quote and the punctuation mark.

Tenses

Broadly speaking, the tense of a verb shows *when* an action, feeling or process happens. If you are referring to an event that happened in the past and is now finished, then clearly the *past* tense is most appropriate:

Louis Armstrong **was born** in New Orleans in 1901.

Tchaikovsky **wrote** *Eugene Onegin* between 1877 and 1878.

Rodgers and Hammerstein's *Oklahoma* **was** first **staged** in New York in 1943.

However, the use of tenses is not quite as straightforward as this might suggest. In particular, the present tense has a number of applications in addition simply to describing what is happening *now at this very moment*. It can be used to describe something that happened or was done in the past as though it were going on now. This use is called the 'historic present', and in writing about music (or about art, or about what someone else has written) you will frequently find it more natural to use the historic present than the past tense. For instance, the beginning of an essay about Vaughan Williams's *The Lark Ascending* might read as follows:

Vaughan Williams **wrote** *The Lark Ascending* in 1914. He **uses** the timbre of the violin to represent the lark.

As you can see, in the first sentence the writer has used the past tense, because the writing of the piece is an event or process that happened once and is now over. But in the second sentence, rather than saying that 'Vaughan Williams *used* the timbre of the violin', the writer shifts to the historic present, because one of the formal elements of the work, the use of timbre, is being described, and this is something that continues to be a living part of the work.

The next example refers back to what was said by a sixteenth-century writer on music, Ganassi. It is taken from Howard Mayer Brown's 1976 book *Embellishing 16th-Century Music*:

Although Ganassi devotes almost his entire treatise on the recorder to *passaggi*, he does say near the end of it that the easiest ornaments of all are *tremoli*, by which he means the grace that we would call trill or mordent.

Although Ganassi's discussion of embellishments was clearly written several centuries ago, Howard Mayer Brown is commenting on the *content* of the work, which is something that *continues* to present information to the modern reader as it did to the sixteenth-century reader.

Transliteration

Transliteration is the process of transcribing or adapting the written words of one language to another, when the language you are transcribing from uses a different alphabet from the one that you are transcribing into. This is a problem in all areas of writing, but it is especially acute in music because of the prominence of Russian and Slavonic composers (see 'Cyrillic lettering' above). A rule of thumb that will suffice for the majority of cases is to take the spelling given in *New Grove II* for the name or word you wish to use.

Upper case

See 'Lower case and upper case' above.

Bibliography

Chalker, S., and E. Weiner, *The Oxford Dictionary of English Grammar* (Oxford University Press, 1994; repr. 1999).

Crystal, D., *Rediscover Grammar*, 2nd edn (Harlow, Essex: Longman, 1996).

'Good and Bad English' – grammar and general English language Web site: <http://www.nobunaga.demon.co.uk/htm/english.htm>

The Oxford Dictionary for Writers and Editors (Oxford: Clarendon Press, 1981; repr. 1990).

Seely, J., *The Oxford Guide to Writing and Speaking* (Oxford University Press, 1998).

Trask, R. L., *The Penguin Guide to Punctuation* (London: Penguin, 1997).

Weiner, E. S. C., and A. Delahunty, *The Oxford Guide to English Usage*, 2nd edn (London: BCA, by arrangement with Oxford University Press, 1994; repr. 1999).

Chapter seven

SOME MUSICAL TERMS AND PHRASES

THIS IS a reference source for some of the terms and phrases commonly used in writings about music. It is highly selective and is restricted to:

- musical terms and phrases that are commonly used in, or in association with, descriptive and analytical text;
- abbreviations that are used in tables and lists;
- clarifications of words or terms that are sometimes used confusingly or inaccurately;
- some commonly used reference material (included for convenience and good measure).

The arrangement of the headings is alphabetical. If you have difficulty finding the item you are looking for, use the index at the back of the book to trace it.

Arrangements, transcriptions and editions of music

These words describe processes carried out on a piece of music that already exists. There is not total agreement about how the meaning of the words 'arrangement' and 'transcription' differs. Both denote the process of adapting or re-using pre-existing material. If you are uncertain whether a published piece is an arrangement or a transcription, you should describe it as it is described in the publication. Otherwise the following can serve as rules of thumb:

- Music transferred from one type of notation to another (say from tonic sol-fa or guitar tablature to staff notation), or written down from an oral source (as with a folksong), is a transcription.
- Music transferred from one medium to another (say from string quartet to piano) without any elaboration or other significant changes may also be called a transcription (though many would call this an arrangement).

- Music transferred from one medium to another so as to make a new work – with elaborations, subtractions, new textures and so on – should be called an arrangement.
- Editing is the practice whereby one person prepares the written work of another for performance. Scholarly editions are aimed at giving instructions to performers that will enable them to understand – from the notated music – what the composer originally intended.

The appropriate abbreviations are:

arrangement	arr.	(meaning 'arranged by or for')
transcription	transcr.	(meaning 'transcribed by or for'; *not* 'trans.', which means 'translated by')
edition	edn	
editor	ed.	(meaning 'edited by')
composer	comp.	(meaning 'composed by')

Avant-garde

This is sometimes used wrongly and confused with 'modernist'. It originated as a military term that translates into English as 'advance guard' – the exploratory force that precedes an army, forging the way ahead. The implication is that an 'avant-garde composer', for example, breaks through conventions and adopts new methods that challenge those around him or her. In the middle of the twentieth century Stockhausen was regarded as a composer of avant-garde music. So the term is a description of a radical position taken by some artists/composers relative to the existing practices of their day, rather than a precise definition of a style.

Bar (measure) numbers and systems: using them to identify parts of works

(See also 'Note-value names' below.)

The best way to identify parts of a work is by referring to a recognizable section (such as a movement) and bar numbers:

The heroic theme heard in the previous movement is heard again a tone higher at bar 21 of the Finale. Also, the ostinato accompaniment between bars 32 and 48 is based on the first three notes of this theme.

A 'system' is also a part of a score. It refers to the two or more staves joined together on the left by a brace. So in Fig. 7.1 the box indicates the second system, third bar.

Fig. 7.1   The box identifies the third bar in the second system.

Classical music/Western art music

The phrase 'classical music' is used widely to mean a category of Western music that distinguishes it from, for example, jazz, pop or folk music. It is the style tradition that includes the music of composers such as Bach, Mozart and Stravinsky. It is so commonly understood in this sense that it is proper to use it in this way in many types of (particularly popular) writing. But while it would be pompous to deny the word 'classical' this meaning, this use of the word is problematic. Within their own musical traditions, non-Western cultures have styles that are sometimes described as 'classical' – styles that sound very different from the Western idea of 'classical music' (for example, Indian classical music). Added to this is the problem that within classical music there is an era called 'the Classical period' (this is mentioned under 'Style periods' below). Many academic writers avoid these issues by using the more explicit term 'Western art music' instead of 'classical music'.

Composers' names

Use the spellings given as the main keyword entry (the article headword) for the person in *New Grove II* if you are in doubt or if there are legitimate alternatives. The same applies where a composer is known to have used two different names: so, for example, use Peter Warlock (1894–1930), rather than Philip Heseltine. In *New Grove II* the most relevant name is the one *not* given in square brackets.

Works by partnerships such as Gilbert and Sullivan, and Rodgers and Hammerstein are so familiar that they can be referred to in this way, but both should be given their full names, and other proper conventions should be followed, if their works are being cited formally.

A problem sometimes arises with the possessive form of a composer's name. The possessive form of a name is the form you create by adding an apostrophe and an 's' to indicate the sense of 'belonging to' or 'of' (as in Schubert's 'Trout' Quintet, or Verdi's *Rigoletto*). There is a school of thought that says that when a name ends in an 's' or 'z', the apostrophe alone is sufficient, and there is no need to add an extra 's' (for example: Brahms' Clarinet Quintet, rather than Brahms's Clarinet Quintet). However, it is also perfectly correct to use both the apostrophe and the extra 's', as in 'Berlioz's *Symphonie fantastique*'.

Dating a musical work

When writing about a composer's output, for example, it is helpful to give the dates of compositions. Whether one gives the date when the composition was completed, published or first performed is a perplexing issue upon which opinions differ. It usually depends on the work in question. There can be very good reasons for giving any of these dates in particular circumstances. In *New Grove II*, when a date is placed in brackets after the title of a work in running text, it is usually the date of composition, except in respect of operas, when the date *and place* of first performance is given. (The date is given *before* the place of performance so that it cannot be mistaken for a publication.)

The convention you use must be consistent and clear. It must also be suitable for the works you are dealing with. However, the following are some general guidelines for good practice:

- Give the date of composition (as given in *New Grove II*) in brackets after the title when mentioning the work in the flow of your text.
- Give the date and place of the first performance if you also, or alternatively, need to do so. Avoid ambiguity by making your meaning clear: (first performed 1912, New York).
- There may be good reasons for also, or alternatively, giving the date of publication. If this is the case, give, if possible, the place of publication too: (published Vienna, 1833).
- Some works are revised, and both the original and revised versions are retained in the repertoire. In such cases it is important to state which version you mean – usually by reference to the composition date: Stravinsky, *Petrushka* (1910/11); or: Stravinsky, *Petrushka* (1945 version).

Dynamic markings

See 'Performance directions' below.

Early instruments

The names of early musical instruments should not usually be abbreviated when you are writing about them. Many pre-Classical instruments can legitimately be called by more than one name. Most early musical instruments have an entry in *New Grove II* or the *New Grove Dictionary of Musical Instruments*. In the interests of consistency it is advisable to use the keyword given in *Grove* (for example 'crumhorn' rather than 'crumcorn', and 'shawm' rather than 'shalmuse'). The names of one or two early instruments can cause confusion. For example:

CORNET AND CORNETT/CORNETTO

The cornet and the cornett (sometimes written 'cornetto') are two entirely different instruments. The cornet is a valved brass instrument that was not invented until the nineteenth century (technically a valved post-horn, and originally called the 'cornopean'). The cornett or cornetto is a wooden lip-vibrated instrument that was prevalent from the fifteenth to the late eighteenth century.

SACKBUT

'Sackbut' is what the trombone was called in England before about 1780. Some use this word to describe the early trombone in any country, but strictly this is wrong. My preference is always to use 'trombone' unless you are quoting a source.

FIDDLE/VIOLIN

'Fiddle' is the generic name for bowed string instruments. In modern usage it is associated with folk music, and the orchestral instrument is always called the 'violin'.

FORTEPIANO

See 'Piano/pianoforte/fortepiano' below.

Early music

The term 'early music' has not gained complete clarity despite decades of custom and practice. It was originally used to mean music of a certain *period* of Western music history, roughly that between and including the medieval and Baroque eras. However, the journal *Early Music* regularly carries articles about music of the Classical period too. This is because the term also suggests an approach to performance that is sympathetic to the styles, conditions and conventions that prevailed when the music was first heard. These values are better covered by other terms such as 'historically-aware' or 'period' performance. (See also 'Historic and historical' below.)

Edition

See 'Arrangements, transcriptions and editions of music' above.

Figured bass and roman-numeral chord symbols

Figured bass used in written text should ideally appear as it does in notated music:

$\frac{5}{3}$ $\frac{6}{4}$ not 'five three, six four'

However, word-processing packages may not have a facility for doing this, so a pragmatic solution would be to separate the figures with a forward slash (/). For example:

The song was almost entirely harmonized with 5/3 and 6/4 chords.

Roman-numeral chord abbreviations should be written as follows:

Major	(upper case)	I–V–I etc.
Minor	(lower case)	I–ii–I–vi etc.
Diminished	(lower case with superscript °)	I–vi–vii° etc.
Augmented	(upper case with superscript +)	i–V–III+ etc.

Inversions can be indicated with letters or figures (the bracketed letters and figures are usually omitted in notated music):

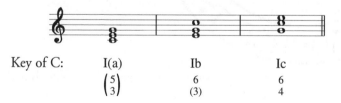

Key of C:	I(a)	Ib	Ic
	$\left(\begin{smallmatrix}5\\3\end{smallmatrix}\right)$	6	6
		(3)	4

A series of chord symbols should be written so that the chords are joined by dashes. For example:

The chord pattern I–IV–iib–V^7–I appears at bars 12–13.

Form analysis: how to describe with letters

Letters are sometimes used in text to describe musical forms. Care should be taken that there is no confusion between such letters and those that indicate pitches. This is usually easy to do. Adjacent letters need not be separated by a space or joined by a dash:

> The first movement follows the typical ABA ternary-form pattern. The B section begins at bar 17.

Genres

Words that denote genres (symphony, concerto, sonata, quartet, quintet and so on) are neither italicized nor given upper-case initial letters unless the title of a specific work is referred to:

> Mozart wrote many piano sonatas, symphonies and concertos.
> Perhaps the best known of his symphonies is the Symphony No. 41 in C (K. 551), also known as the 'Jupiter' Symphony.

(More information on the correct way to cite musical works is given in Chapter 10.)

There is seldom a need to abbreviate words such as symphony and concerto in written text. However, abbreviations are usually appropriate when a word is being used several times in succession – for example, in a list of works or a table. The list below gives the commonly used abbreviations for genres.

concerto	conc.
overture	ov.
quartet	qt
quintet	qnt
symphony	symph. or sym.

The plurals 'concertos' and 'concerti' are equally legitimate, but the plural of 'concerto grosso' is 'concerti grossi'.
(See also 'Mass/oratorio' below.)

Harmonic series and 'natural' notes

Most brass players recognize the term 'harmonic series' as meaning the notes that can be produced without using valves or a slide. The harmonic series is illustrated in Ex. 7.1. Sometimes it is necessary to distinguish between the notes of a given series and those that lie outside that series – when discussing Baroque instruments, for example. There is no standard way of doing this, but 'natural notes' can be used for the notes of the harmonic series, and 'non-natural' notes for those outside a given series.

Ex. 7.1   Harmonic series on C. The pitches in the harmonic series only approximate to the notes shown. The darkened notes (B♭, F♯ and so on) are particularly out of tune in equal temperament. For this reason these 'notes' are sometimes referred to as 'tones'.

Historic and historical

An 'historic' instrument is a surviving specimen of an old form of an instrument. An 'historical' instrument is a modern instrument that is copied from or inspired by an older model.

Horn

'Horn' is sometimes used in jazz parlance to mean any brass or, indeed, wind instrument. In writing, it is best to specify the actual instrument in question, unless you are really referring to the orchestral (french) horn.

The term 'french horn' should be spelled with a lower-case 'f', not as 'French horn'. Similarly 'english horn', if it is used in preference to 'cor anglais', should be spelled with a lower-case 'e'.

Inscriptions and other markings on musical instruments

See Chapter 5, page 89.

Keys

The forms given here for describing keys are widely accepted, but they are not the only patterns that can be used:

C major and C minor *or* C maj. and C min.

Never mix the two forms in one piece of writing.

When a sharp or flat is used as part of a pitch name it can be written as a symbol – for example, F♯ – or the word 'flat' or 'sharp' can be written out:

Sonata in E♭ major, Op. 27 No. 1
Sonata in E flat major, Op. 27 No. 1

Mass/oratorio

A mass is not an oratorio – it is a setting of the Roman Catholic rite, whereas an oratorio is more broadly a musical treatment of a text based on a religious theme. A mass should not be referred to as a type of oratorio.

Modes

The names of modes are given in roman with a capital letter to start.

Dvořák frequently used modal tunes. In the second movement he introduces a melody in the Dorian mode based on a Czech folksong.

The modes as they relate to the white notes of a piano keyboard are:

Ionian   starting on C
Dorian   starting on D
Phrygian   starting on E
Lydian   starting on F
Mixolydian   starting on G
Aeolian   starting on A
Locrian   starting on B

Musical instruments and voice types – their names and abbreviations

The names of instruments are not italicized when given in the usual English form. If there are special reasons for writing the name in the foreign-language equivalent, then that foreign word is italicized; for example, 'bassoon' is given in roman, but *fagotto* (Italian) and *basson* (French) are italic in English-language writings. The English-language name for an instrument can be used, irrespective of how it is represented in a score. So, for example, one can refer to 'Verdi's bassoon parts' even though they are labelled '*fagotti*' in his scores. The abbreviated names of instruments are usually only used for lists, tables and in notated music. The abbreviations shown in Table 7.1 are the ones used in *New Grove II*.

Natural instruments

'Natural trumpets' and 'natural horns' are instruments that have no valves or other mechanical features.

'Natural' notes

See 'Harmonic series and "natural" notes' above.

Note-value names (crotchets, quarter notes, etc.)

The terms used for describing rhythmic values are different in the UK and USA. Whether you use the British or American system depends on whether you are required to use one or the other, and on which is most commonly encountered in the country for which you are writing. Obviously you should use your chosen system consistently unless you are quoting someone who uses a different system.

The equivalent terms and note values are as follows:

British	*American*
time signature	meter signature
bar	measure
breve	breve (or double whole-note)
semibreve	whole note
minim	half note
crotchet	quarter note
quaver	eighth note
semiquaver	sixteenth note
demisemiquaver	thirty-second note
hemidemisemiquaver	sixty-fourth note

Table 7.1   **Abbreviations for instruments and voices given in** *New Grove*

A	alto [voice]	mar	marimba
a	alto [instrument]	Mez	mezzo-soprano
acc.	accompaniment,	mic	microphone
	accompanied by	mod	modulator
accdn	accordion	nar	narrator
amp	amplified	ob	oboe
B	bass [voice]	obbl	obbligato
b	bass [instrument]	orch	orchestra, orchestral
Bar	baritone [voice]	org	organ
bar	baritone [instrument]	perc	percussion
B-Bar	bass-baritone	pf	piano
bc	basso continuo	pic	piccolo
bn	bassoon	prep pf	prepared piano
C	contralto	rec	recorder
cel	celesta	S	soprano [voice]
chit	chitarrone	s	soprano [instrument]
chmb	chamber	S,A,T,B	solo voices
cimb	cimbalom	SATB	chorus
cl	clarinet	sax	saxophone
clvd	clavichord	spkr	speaker
cont	continuo	str	string(s)
Ct	countertenor	synth	synthesizer
db	double bass	T	tenor [voice]
dbn	double bassoon	t	tenor [instrument]
el	electric	timp	timpani
el-ac	electroacoustic	tpt	trumpet
elec	electronic	Tr	treble [voice]
eng hn	english horn	tr	treble [instrument]
ens	ensemble	trbn	trombone
fl	flute	unacc.	unaccompanied
glock	glockenspiel	v, vv	voice(s)
gui	guitar	va	viola
hmn	harmonium	vc	cello
hn	horn	vib	vibraphone
hp	harp	vle	violone
hpd	harpsichord	vn	violin
inst(s)	instrument(s), instrumental	ww	woodwind
kbd	keyboard	xyl	xylophone
mand	mandolin		

(*Grove* punctuates only the abbreviations 'acc.' and 'unacc.'. For standard conventions for punctuating abbreviations, see Chapter 6, 'Abbreviations'.)

Oratorio

See 'Mass/oratorio' above.

Orchestra and voices: the order in which performers are listed

Performers are usually acknowledged in the programmes of orchestral concerts (as are chorus members). The following order for instruments is commonly used:

1st violin	Flute	Horn	Timpani	Keyboards	Harp
2nd violin	Piccolo	Trumpet	Percussion		
Viola	Oboe	Trombone			
Cello	Cor anglais	Bass trombone			
Double Bass	Clarinet	Tuba			
	Bass clarinet				
	Bassoon				
	Contrabassoon				

The leader or 'concertmaster' is usually acknowledged as such at the start of the list of first violins, and section principals are acknowledged with the word 'principal' in brackets after their names.

Solo singers are usually given prominence (along with the conductor) in programme and liner notes. Both soloists and choristers are listed from the highest voice to the lowest. For example: soprano (or treble, as appropriate), alto, tenor, baritone, bass.

Performance directions

By 'performance directions' I mean dynamic markings such as *fortissimo, mezzo-piano* and *forte* and tempo marks such as *andante, presto* and *larghetto*, as well as instructions such as *pesante, forza, stringendo* and *energico*.

There are two schools of thought about whether or not performance directions should be given in italics or roman lettering. Most pieces of music have performance directions in languages other than English, and so there is a good argument for treating such directions as foreign words and putting them in italics. However, many terms are so basic to the language of music and writings about music that there is no need to treat them as foreign. (This distinction is addressed in a more general context in Chapter 6, under 'Foreign words' and 'Foreign words that have been anglicized'.)

As you can see from the examples in the first paragraph above, I feel that it is best to give performance directions in italics. Indeed, for the sake of clarity and consistency I would do this even when the directions are given in English. When used in written text, they stand out more clearly from the words around them if they are italicized, and this can help make the sense of a sentence immediately clear.

When a tempo or expression mark is used as a point of reference in a work you should italicize it:

> Verdi used many devices for changing moods. For example, the mood becomes more tense at the *Andante* because the harmonies are richer and more complex.

If you are using the term generally, it is given in italics and lower case:

> Trumpets and horns are prominent in the last movements of Mahler's symphonies. He seldom uses brass in *andante* passages.

However, when such a term forms the *title of a movement*, it is usual practice to give it in roman, with an initial capital letter and without quotes (see Chapter 10):

> The Andante largo of Corelli's Concerto No. 11 in B flat major

Abbreviations of performance directions should also be italicized:

forte	*f*
mezzo-forte	*mf*
pianissimo	*pp*
rinforzando	*rf* or *rfz*
sforzando or sforzato	*sf* or *sfz*

Generally, such abbreviations should not contain full stops, but there are a few exceptions to this. These include:

da capo	*D.C.*
dal segno	*D.S.*

and any abbreviation formed when a term is shortened to its first three or more letters, such as:

accelerando	*accel.*
ad libitum	*ad lib.*
crescendo	*cresc.*
diminuendo	*dim.*
espressivo	*espress.* or *espr.*
rallentando	*rall.*

ritardando	rit. or ritard.
ritenuto	rit. or riten.
staccato	stacc.

Period performance

In a period performance one would expect to hear historical or even historic instruments (see above), and an attempt to observe the performance conventions that applied when the work in question was written.

Piano/pianoforte/fortepiano

'Piano' is the accepted term for pianoforte, and it should be used except when 'pianoforte' appears in a passage you want to quote. 'Fortepiano' is often used to denote the late eighteenth- or early nineteenth-century species of instrument. This too should only be used when it is being quoted, or when you really are referring to an historic instrument (see above) or a reproduction of one.

Pitch classes

A pitch class is a pitch name (see below) that is not specific to a particular octave. So, for example, the pitch class 'C' refers to all notes called 'C' and not just to middle C. Table 7.2 shows the systems for pitch classes in the main European languages. In written text, however, the English names can be used unless there is a particular need to use one of the other languages – for example, if you were using a quotation. In German there are some exceptions that apply to pitch classes with accidentals: these include *B* for B flat (the pitch B is given as *H* in German), *Es* for E flat and *As* for A flat.

Pitch names

Note names should usually be given in upper-case letters. Often, one need only mention a pitch class (see above). For example:

The clarinet plays the repeated quavers on D that were heard four bars earlier on the flute.

Table 7.2   **Pitch classes**

English	C	D	E	F	G	A	B
German	*C*	*D*	*E*	*F*	*G*	*A*	*H*
French	*ut*	*ré*	*mi*	*fa*	*sol*	*la*	*si*
Italian	*do*	*re*	*mi*	*fa*	*sol*	*la*	*si*
Spanish	*do*	*re*	*mi*	*fa*	*sol*	*la*	*si*

	C sharp	C flat	C double sharp	C double flat
English	C sharp	C flat	C double sharp	C double flat
German	*Cis*	*Ces*	*Cisis*	*Ceses*
French	*ut dièse*	*ut bémol*	*ut double-dièse*	*ut double-bémol*
Italian	*do diesis*	*do bemolle*	*do doppio diesis*	*do doppio bemolle*
Spanish	*do sostenido*	*do bemol*	*do doble sostenido*	*do doble bemol*

However, pitch names are also used in written text to denote exact pitch without using music notation. Sometimes, for example, they are used to describe the range of an instrument or the *tessitura* (see 'Tessitura and range' below) of a song. There are several systems for doing this, but the two most commonly used are the Helmholtz system and the American Standard system. *New Grove II* uses a version of the Helmholtz system, but I greatly prefer the American Standard system, which also seems to be favoured by musical acousticians.

HELMHOLTZ SYSTEM

In this system (Ex. 7.2a) a combination of upper- and lower-case letters in italics, and primes are used to represent pitches.

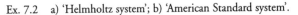

Ex. 7.2   a) 'Helmholtz system'; b) 'American Standard system'.

Ａmerican Ｓtandard Ｓystem
In this system (Ex. 7.2b) middle C is called C_4, and $A_4 = 440Hz$. The octave C_0 to B_0 includes the lowest pitches that are audible to humans, and C_9 to B_9 the highest notes ever written in Western music.

Irrespective of which pitch-name system you use, when you give a series of pitch names in written text, they should be joined by dashes. For example:

B–f–d

or

$F\sharp_4–A_4–B_5$

Popular and 'pop'

'Popular music' can have a number of meanings. It can simply mean music that has mass appeal:

> The concert included some of the most popular music from operas, including excerpts from *La bohème*.

It can also mean a type of music that is different from 'art' or 'classical' music:

> As a student he studied Mozart and Haydn, but he became a specialist in popular music after developing an interest in folksong and jazz.

'Pop' music however has taken on a particular meaning. It is a species of popular music, but it has come to mean music that is aimed at youth culture:

> Elton John was educated at the Royal Academy of Music, before going on to become one of the most successful British pop singer/composers.

'Problem' words

Check spellings of which you are uncertain in a good music dictionary, but take particular care with the following, which are often misspelled:

a cappella	Liszt
acciaccatura	Mendelssohn
anacrusis	*Missa solemnis*

appoggiatura	mordent
ballade	obbligato
capriccio	prima donna
intermezzo	scherzo

Range

See 'Tessitura and range' below.

Record, recording, disc, disk or CD

The word 'recording' is best used to describe the *process* of recording, but when referring to recorded sound it is easier and clearer to refer to the particular medium in question:

> Elvis made several recordings that he would be less proud of than others. But some of his early 45rpm discs are as revealing of the individuality of his singing style as any. Many of these early recordings are now available on compilation CDs.

'Disk' is an American spelling of 'disc', but also a shortened version of 'diskette', which is a computer floppy disk. You can avoid confusion by using the spelling 'disc' for audio recordings.

Religious, sacred and liturgical music

'Religious' and 'sacred' can be used to describe music of any appropriate type and culture. However, it is most common for Western art-music settings of a religious text to be referred to as 'sacred music'. 'Liturgical' has a more precise meaning: it should only be used to describe music that is a setting of a part of a religious *service* or *ritual*.

Score, parts, system and related words

A score is the paper copy of a musical work that contains all the parts to be played or sung. A score may be written in its full form (full score) or in a condensed form (a short score, or vocal score). The paper copy of the music to be played or sung by an individual performer is usually referred to as a 'part'. For example:

> The conductor checked the score and found that all the clarinet parts had been wrongly transposed.

The group of five horizontal lines on which notes are written is the staff or stave. A system is a group of staves (or staffs) joined together by a brace. See also 'Bar numbers and systems' above.

Style periods (Renaissance, Baroque, Classical etc.)

The factors that explain periods in Western music history are discussed in many textbooks and dictionaries. The approximate dates when the main style periods prevailed are given below (these terms and dates apply to music, but not necessarily to other arts, even though, for example, the word 'Renaissance' is applied to paintings and to music); however, there are dangers in using periodizations. Among these dangers are two that should always be kept in mind:

* Style periods are not joined end to end as if there were a consensus among composers that the Classical period, for example, should stop on one day and the Romantic period start the day after – this idea is as absurd as it sounds. Style periods overlapped, and the identifying ingredients of each took some time to establish themselves. Most such periods acquired many years later the names we now use for them.
* Style periods are identified in broad chronological terms. But this does not mean that every composer who lived in a particular period can be described merely in terms of the label given to that style period. For example, Elgar lived until 1934, but few think of him as a modern or Modernist composer.

The style period labels in most common use are given below. Each date is preceded by the abbreviation *c.* (*circa*) meaning 'around', or 'about' – and these dates really are approximate; musicologists do not agree about them.

The Renaissance period	*c.*1450–*c.*1600
The Baroque period	*c.*1600–*c.*1750
The Classical period	*c.*1750–*c.*1820
The Romantic period	*c.*1820–*c.*1900
The Modern period	*c.*1900–

Tempo marks

See 'Performance directions' above.

Tessitura and range

The range (or compass) of an instrument or voice is the distance between the lowest and highest note normally available on that instrument or voice. Tessitura is the part of the range that is written for in a particular piece. So, a piece of music in which the higher notes of an instrument or voice are continuously exploited could be said to use a 'high tessitura'.

Textures

The adjectives from polyphony, counterpoint and homophony that can be used to describe texture are respectively 'polyphonic', 'contrapuntal' and 'homophonic'.

'Polyphony' and 'counterpoint' have virtually the same meaning, but polyphony is more frequently used of medieval and Renaissance music, and counterpoint is applied to later music:

> The stunning feature of Palestrina's sacred vocal music is the rich polyphonic texture.

but

> Bach's mastery of counterpoint makes him stand out among Baroque composers.

'Homophony' can mean a strictly chordal texture (as with a hymn) in which the melodic interest is in one (usually the highest) line, but it can also refer to a clearly-defined melody-plus-accompaniment texture. The use of the term 'melody/accompaniment' for the latter would make the meaning clearer.

Time signatures

In published books or articles, time signatures are usually set as they look in notated music, that is, with the two figures directly over each other, not as a fraction – *not* ¾, for example. This is difficult or impossible to type on a word processor, so if you are typing it is best to give time signatures as figures joined by a hyphen ('The opening of the work is in 3-4 time'). This, incidentally, is the method that many publishers prefer when receiving copy in electronic form. If, when writing descriptive or analytical text, there is a risk of confusion between figured bass and time signatures, it is best to distinguish between the two by putting the time signature in bold type.

Tonic sol-fa

John Curwen's system is properly written as 'tonic sol-fa'. The full range of symbols with their equivalents as degrees of the major scale is given in Table 7.3. When given in written text the symbols should be lower case and italic. A series of symbols (with no intention to denote rhythmic value) should be joined by dashes:

> Morgan used to precede rehearsals with warming-up exercises. The bass section would sing *doh*, and they would be joined by the other voices singing the notes of the common chord. When *doh–me–soh* were perfectly in tune, he would commence the rehearsal.

Table 7.3   **Tonic sol-fa names and their scale degree equivalents**

doh	*ray*	*me*	*fah*
tonic	supertonic	mediant	subdominant
(1st)	(2nd)	(3rd)	(4th)
soh	*lah*	*te*	*doh*
dominant	submediant	leading-note	tonic
(5th)	(6th)	(7th)	(8th/1st)

Transcription

See 'Arrangements, transcriptions and editions of music' above.

Transposing instruments

The key in which a transposing instrument is pitched should always be given when quoting a music extract. However, in written text this may not be necessary. In general, the pitch class of an instrument should be quoted if:

- it is not one of the most standard pitches and it is important to distinguish it (for example, clarinet in E flat, or trumpet in F);
- the reference is linked to a quoted music extract. For example:

> This can be seen in the high writing for the E flat clarinet that is given in Ex. 9.

- to do otherwise would weaken the meaning of your writing or make it less clear.

'Horn in F' or 'Clarinet in A' is better than 'the F Horn' or 'the A Clarinet', but either system is acceptable if it is used consistently.

Voices and their abbreviations

See 'Musical instruments and voice types – their names and abbreviations' above.

Words set to music: libretto, lyric, text or vocals

The words that are sung to music can often be appropriately referred to simply as 'the words'. Beyond that, the following might serve as a rule of thumb:
- Libretto is the words of an opera.
- Lyrics are the words set to music in popular songs and shows.
- Texts are words set to music in other genres. For example, you should refer to the words of liturgical works not as librettos or lyrics but as texts.
- Vocals is the term often used to describe the sung parts in pop music.

Bibliography

Boustead, A., *Writing Down Music* (Oxford University Press, 1975).
Holoman, D. K., *Writing about Music: A Style Sheet from the Editors of 19th-Century Music* (Berkeley: University of California Press, 1988).
Randel, D. M. (ed.), *The New Harvard Dictionary of Music* (Cambridge, Mass.: Belknap Press; Harvard University Press, 1986).
Read, G., *Music Notation: A Manual of Modern Practice*, 2nd edn (Boston, Mass.: Allyn & Bacon, 1969; repr. by Taplinger Publishing Company, New York, 1979).
Strahle, G., *An Early Music Dictionary: Musical terms from British sources 1500–1740* (Cambridge University Press, 1995).

Chapter eight

SOURCES AND RESEARCH TOOLS

THIS CHAPTER is about the books and electronic resources you can use to find information about music. 'Research tools' include reference works such as dictionaries, encyclopedias, catalogues and bibliographies. Some reference books, such as shorter dictionaries, have a limited purpose: they provide accurate information about the meanings and spellings of common and more unusual words. But some are also 'research tools'; they have more ambitious and sometimes more specialized functions. As well as answering direct questions they provide information that allows readers to progress further in finding out about a subject. Even if you only need to consult books for reference purposes, it is advisable to be aware of the many more specialist books that music researchers use. Often, apparently simple questions cannot be answered by looking at the more general reference works. For this reason, even though this chapter is about the problems faced by academic researchers, the information it contains is pertinent to anyone who needs to find information about music.

Irrespective of why you seek information, you need to give careful thought to what exactly you are looking for: to define your investigation into a series of questions. This is important, not just because it helps you to approach your task with a clear focus, but also because it imposes a discipline upon you. It encourages you to seek information purposefully and to avoid meandering in the maze of seductive byways that reference and research books and the World Wide Web can lead you to. This, by the way, is a temptation that every researcher, no matter how experienced, is susceptible to. It does not mean that your area of investigation has to be pared down to absolute factual basics to which you stick rigidly. One of the most interesting aspects of research is that the very process of doing it leads you to unexpected information that stimulates you, feeds your curiosity and allows you to see your topic in a new light. But this happens most positively when your point of departure and the main path that you follow are well defined and systematically organized.

Different types of music and literature about music

There are many different types of music, and various perspectives from which they can be investigated. As lines of investigation have been developed by specialists, they have attracted distinctive styles of analysis, criticism and scholarship. Thus the best histories of different kinds of music and the debates about them are in specialist books and reference materials. However, this does not mean that different categories of music are permanently separate and pigeon-holed. Indeed, one of the most interesting and enriching aspects of more recent music study is the extent to which different types of music have been shown to relate to each other, and how the techniques for studying ethnomusicology, say, shed light on Western traditions. However, as I suggest below, the sources for finding the information you want about particular areas of music may well be reference works that were assembled to meet the needs of the specialist.

Music and the literatures of other subjects

Music is not isolated from the rest of human endeavour, and the work of historians, sociologists, economists, anthropologists, biographers, art historians and others can inform our understanding of music and sometimes provide answers to frustrating questions of detail. Libraries are full of books and other media that are helpful to music research. But many of them have not been designed primarily with musicians in mind. So how do you find the books that you need – books that will provide the answers you are looking for and feed your curiosity and imagination – when you do not know that they exist, or at least do not know what they are called?

In this chapter I suggest some basic reference works that are useful to musicians, but my list is far from comprehensive. New books are constantly being published, and in the twenty-first century what is sometimes referred to as 'the knowledge revolution', a phenomenon brought about by the development of the Internet and its attendant electronic devices, provides new and diverse ways of accessing knowledge. But these developments, while they have genuinely revolutionized opportunities for those who seek knowledge, also bring challenges. Indeed – and this is a point that cannot be over-emphasized – the knowledge revolution has not, in itself, provided a significantly new *body* of knowledge in music or the arts in general; it has revolutionized the way we *access* the knowledge that is already in place. Provided that you have the necessary equipment and the skills with which to use it, you can obtain information irrespective of where you live. But because this information is so easily available, it is important to be able to discern the difference between what is authoritative and reliable, and what is not. This is why I emphasized in Chapter 3 the need for the World Wide Web to be used as discriminatingly as one would use a library full of books.

It is also important to emphasize the value to a research project of properly acquired and recorded oral sources. Under 'oral sources' I include recorded interviews with, for example, composers, performers and others. The information gained from well-conducted interviews can be extremely useful.

However, my point of departure in this chapter is the printed word. I have adopted this approach largely because I believe that the skills of research are best learned – at least initially – by using printed material, as this is the basis for most scholarly knowledge about music. Many databases available through the Internet, such as that of *New Grove II*, are based on digitized versions of reference works originally or simultaneously published as books.

Research and reference tools

Research and reference tools are books or the equivalent of books in other media – such as CD-ROMs, Web sites and microfiche sets. Good research tools have the following qualities:

- They provide definitive information on matters of factual accuracy in their own right. This may be on matters such as the dates of events, the spelling or meanings of words, the location of a venue and so on; or on more substantial matters such as comprehensive information about the lives of people, the works of a composer, or the history and design of a musical instrument.
- They provide information about other relevant sources.
- They are (usually) updated periodically to take account of new data, information and scholarly opinions.

A dictionary is a research tool because it provides information about the meanings of words and the way that they can be applied. But not all dictionaries are as comprehensive as others. For example, the *Oxford English Dictionary* (*OED*) in its complete form (as opposed to its abbreviated forms such as the 'Shorter' and 'Pocket' versions) runs to twenty volumes. It gives not just the spellings and meanings of words but a wealth of information about how those words have been used through the ages. Anyone researching into the violin, for example, will find pages of information about how that word has been used since the sixteenth century and the sources for that information (see Fig. 8.1). Thus, *OED* provides information about a range of historical sources that might not otherwise have occurred to you.

A note on editions and media

Some reference and research tools are listed below; but I should offer a qualifying remark about this information. The details are accurate at the time that this book is being assembled. But, as I have said, one of the features of really good research tools is that they are regularly updated. As a general rule, you should use the latest available edition of whatever source is mentioned.

Research tools may also take the form of Web sites or CD-ROMs, as well as printed books. For example, *New Grove II* is available in printed and on-line forms. *Encyclopaedia Britannica* and the *Oxford English Dictionary* are also available in electronic form. Sometimes the CD-ROMs are available for use in public or institutional libraries, but increasingly they are also available through the Internet. But remember that it is impossible to anticipate changes that the owners of individual sites may make and when they will make them. Do not be too surprised if you find that a site does not work or the URL you have typed in is re-directed.

Two important sources

Two texts have a special place in music reference and research: the latest edition of *The New Grove Dictionary of Music and Musicians*, now known as *New Grove II*, and the latest (5th) edition of Vincent Duckles's *Music Reference and Research Materials: An Annotated Bibliography*. It is worth giving a brief explanation of why these two works are so important and how they are laid out.

Entry printed from *Oxford English Dictionary Online* © Oxford University Press 2001

violin, *n.*   SECOND EDITION
                                                        1989

(vaɪə'lɪn, 'vaɪəlɪn) Forms: 6 **violine**, 7 **vyoline**, **viallin**, 7- **violin**. [ad. It. *violino* (Pg. *violino*, Sp. *violin*), f. *viola* VIOLA². Cf. VIOLON.]

1. a. A musical instrument in common use, having four strings tuned in fifths and played with a bow; a fiddle.

In general structure the violin is composed of a resonant box of elaborately curved outline, and a neck or handle from the end of which the strings are stretched over a bridge to a tail-piece.

1579 SPENSER *Sheph. Cal., April* 103, I see Calliope speede her to the place, where my Goddesse shines: And after her the other Muses trace, with their Violines. **1589** R. HARVEY *Pl. Perc.* (1590) 6 Then were it high time for..all Peace-Makers, to put vp their pipes, or else in steed of the soft violine, learne to sound a shrill trumpet. **1608** B. JONSON *Masques* Wks. (1616) 964 The first [dance] was to the Cornets, the second to the Vyolines. **1618** BOLTON *Florus* (1636) 115 Some excellently pleasing lesson plaid upon soft winde-instruments, or Violins. **1660** PEPYS *Diary* 6 Mar., I played upon a viall, and he a viallin, after dinner. **1711** STEELE *Spect.* No. 258 ¶4 Violins, Voices, or any other Organs of Sound. **1756-7** tr. *Keysler's Trav.* (1760) II. 10 Orpheus or Amphion in bronze, playing upon a violin. **1842** LYTTON *Zanoni* I. i, He was not only a composer, but also an excellent practical performer, especially on the violin. **1884** HAWEIS *My Musical Life* I. 237 The violin is not an invention, it is a growth.

transf. **1670** EACHARD *Cont. Clergy* 62 People..presently phansi'd the Moon, Mercury, and Venus to be a kind of violins or trebles to Jupiter and Saturn.

b. With distinguishing terms.

1601 B. JONSON *Poetast.* III. iv, Come, we must haue you turne fiddler againe, slaue, 'get a base violin at your backe. *c*1670 WOOD *Life* (O.H.S.) I. 212 Before the restoration of K. Charles 2 and especially after, viols began to be out of fashion, and only violins used, as treble-violin, tenor and bass-violin. **1685** PLAYFORD (*title*), The Division-Violin: containing a Collection of Divisions upon several Grounds for the Treble-Violin. **1728** CHAMBERS *Cycl.* s.v., The Word Violin, alone, stands for Treble Violin. *Ibid.*, The Counter-Tenor, Tenor, or Bass-Violin. **1888** *Encycl. Brit.* XXIV. 245/1 The tenor violin, in compass a fifth lower than the treble violin, appears to have preceded the latter.

c. *to play first violin*, to take the leading part. (Cf. FIDDLE *n.* 1b.) Similarly (*rare*), **to**

Fig. 8.1   Part of the *Oxford English Dictionary Online* entry on 'Violin'. The entry contains a definition of 'violin' and a series of examples of how the word has been used since 1579.

The New Grove Dictionary of Music and Musicians, second edition (New Grove II)

Sadie, Stanley (ed.), *The New Grove Dictionary of Music and Musicians*, 2nd edn, 29 vols (London: Macmillan; New York: Grove's Dictionaries, 2001).

This is the most authoritative and wide-ranging English-language dictionary of music. The present edition was published in 2001, and while it is the second edition of what is now called *New Grove*, it is actually the seventh edition to carry the title *Grove*. Publication of the first edition commenced in 1879.

The status of *New Grove II* in music research and reference is undisputed, and though it is edited and published in the UK, scholars from around the world contribute articles to it and it is distributed internationally. Most of the articles have common features, and it is worth being aware of these to get the most from *Grove*:

- The title of the article or entry, followed by alternative names or spellings (see Fig. 8.2). For example, the name of an instrument is normally given in English, followed by the other names by which the instrument is known.
- If an article is about a person, the places and dates of birth and death are given, followed by a brief explanation of that person's significance (see Fig. 8.3).
- The title word (article headword) for concepts, movements, institutions and so on is followed by a brief definition.
- The article itself. Some articles are divided into several sections under headings that suit the subject. Articles vary in length: some are a paragraph long, others run to several thousand words.
- For composers there may be a list of works. These work-lists are extremely important because they are usually comprehensive and, in the case of major composers, they include information about dates of composition and first performances, and about keys and thematic catalogue numbers (see Fig. 8.4).
- For persons there may also be a 'Writings' section that gives details of books and articles they have written.
- Bibliography. Almost every entry has a bibliography arranged in chronological order. This contains a selection of the most important and trusted works published about the subject of the

entry. (It is worth noting that the style of *Grove* bibliographies differs from both the short-title and the author–date systems: it is a little less detailed, giving the author name – initial first – followed by the title, and the place and date of publication.)

- Author's name. The name of the contributor(s) appears at the end of an article. Many articles were written for an earlier edition and were subsequently revised, either by the same author or by someone else. All contributors' names are given.

Grove is important not just because of its rigour, detail and authority, but also because of the vastness of its scope: it is the most comprehensive reference work about music in any language – probably more so than its only serious rival, the highly respected multi-volume German encyclopedia *Die Musik in Geschichte und Gegenwart: Allgemeine Enzyklopädie der Musik*. *Grove* has entries for composers, performers, instruments, genres and musical terms. But there are also

Rondeña. Song and group dance of Andalusian origin and flamenco type. (*See* FLAMENCO, Table 1, and SPAIN, §II, 4.

A cross reference

Subject

Rondo (It., also Eng. and Ger. by usage; Fr. *rondeau*). One of the most fundamental designs in music, the rondo is a structure consisting of a series of sections, the first of which (the main section or refrain) recurs, normally in the home key, between subsidiary sections (*couplets*, episodes) before returning finally to conclude, or round off, the composition (*ABAC ... A*).

Alternative spelling

1. Origins and development of the formal concept. 2. The rondeau in France in the 17th and early 18th centuries. 3. The spread of the rondo. 4. The rondos of C.P.E. Bach. 5. The rondo as a movement in a larger work. 6. The sonata-rondo. 7. The independent rondo. 8. The rondo in the 19th and 20th centuries.

Plan for the article

1. ORIGINS AND DEVELOPMENT OF THE FORMAL CONCEPT. The very simplicity of the rondo concept, and its consequent wide usage, makes it difficult to give a precise account of its origins. Any connection between the medieval or Renaissance rondeau and that of the 17th and 18th centuries is at best tenuous; and parallels between the later rondo and (for example) the ritornello principle and the rondo cantata need to be more thoroughly investigated. Those for 18th-century theorists

Fig. 8.2   The *New Grove II* entry for Rondeña and part of Rondo.

ASTA-ROSE ALCAIDE/ALEXANDRE DELGADO

Subject — (Sousa, John Philip) (*b* Washington DC, 6 Nov 1854; *d* Reading, PA, 6 March 1932). American composer, bandmaster and author. Composer of the official national march of the United States, *The Stars and Stripes Forever*, Sousa, who was known as the 'March King', was the most important figure in the history of bands and band music.

Brief detail of subject

Plan of the entry — 1. Life. 2. Legacy. 3. Works.

1. LIFE. Both his parents were immigrants: his father, John Antonio, a trombonist in the US Marine Band, was born in Spain of Portuguese parents; his mother, Marie Elisabeth Trinkaus, was born in Bavaria. The family name was Sousa, despite stories that it was originally 'So', to

Sousa wished to keep them exclusively for his own band, ten and few were published. oor

WORKS — **Work-list**
Unless otherwise stated, printed works were published in Philadelphia, and MSS of unpublished works are in US-Wc

for a more complete list of works see GroveA (H.W. Hitchcock)

STAGE
operettas unless otherwise stated

Author

The Phoenix (Bohemians and Detectives) (incid music, J. Bludso), 1875, lost
Matt Morgan's Living Pictures (incid music), 1876, Washington DC, 977)
spr. 1876, lost
Katherine (3, W.J. Vance), 1879
Our Flirtations (incid music, Sousa, Vance, E. Bartlett, others, after J.B. Wilson), 1880
Florine (M.A. Denison), 1881, unfinished
The Smugglers (2, Vance, after F.C. Burnand: *The Contrabandista*), 1882, Washington DC, 25 March 1882

J.N. Korzun: *The Orchestral Transcriptions for Band of John Philip Sousa* (diss., U. of Illinois, 1994)
M.E. Hester: *A Study of the Saxophone Soloists Performing with the John Philip Sousa Band: 1893–1930* (diss., U. of Arizona, 1995)
P.E. Bierley: *Sousa Band Fraternal Society News Index* (Westerville, 1997)
A set of 85 scrapbooks containing clippings and programmes of the Sousa Band is in the archives of the US Marine Band, Washington DC.

(PAUL E. BIERLEY)

Fig. 8.3   Extracts from the *New Grove II* entry for a person: John Philip Sousa.

WORKS

Editions: *Ludwig van Beethovens Werke: Vollständige kritisch durchgesehene überall berechtigte Ausgabe*, i–xxiv (Leipzig, 1862–5/R), xxv [suppl.] (Leipzig, 1888) [GA]
Beethoven: Sämtliche Werke: Supplemente zur Gesamtausgabe, ed. W. Hess (Wiesbaden, 1959–71) [HS]
Beethoven: Werke: neue Ausgabe sämtlicher Werke, ed. J. Schmidt-Görg and others (Munich and Duisburg, 1961–) [NA]

Works are identified in the left-hand column by opus and woo (Werk ohne Opuszahl, 'work without opus number') numbers as listed in G. Kinsky and H. Halm: *Das Werk Beethovens* (Munich and Duisburg, 1955) and by Hess numbers as listed in W. Hess: *Verzeichnis der nicht in der Gesamtausgabe veröffentlichten Werke Ludwig van Beethovens* (Wiesbaden, 1957). Works published in GA are identified by the volume in which they appear (roman numeral) and the position in the publisher's continuous numeration (arabic number); works published in HS are listed in the GA column and identified by volume number. Works published in NA are identified by category (roman numeral) and volume within each category (arabic number).

p – *parts*
s – *full score*
vs – *vocal score*

ORCHESTRAL

No.	Title, Key	Composition, First performance	Publication	Dedication, Remarks	GA	NA
op.21	Symphony no.1, C	1799–1800; 2 April 1800	p: Leipzig 1801	Baron Gottfried van Swieten	i/1	i/1
op.36	Symphony no.2, D	1801–2; 5 April 1803	p: Vienna, 1804; for pf, vn, vc: Vienna, 1805	Prince Karl von Lichnowsky	i/2	i/1
op.55	Symphony no.3 'Eroica', E♭	1803; 7 April 1805	p: Vienna, 1806	Prince Franz Joseph von Lobkowitz; 1st private perf. at Lobkowitz palace, sum. 1804	i/3	
op.60	Symphony no.4, B♭	1806; March 1807	p: Vienna, 1808	Count Franz von Oppersdorff	i/4	
op.138	Overture 'Leonore no.1', C	1807; 7 Feb 1828	s, p: Vienna, 1838	for Leonore ovs. nos.2–3, see 'Operas'	iii/19	
op.62	Overture to Collin's Coriolan, c	1807; March 1807	p: Vienna, 1808	Heinrich Joseph von Collin	iii/18	ii/1
op.67	Symphony no.5, c	1807–8; 22 Dec 1808	p: Leipzig, 1809	Prince Lobkowitz and Count Andreas Rasumovsky; preliminary sketches, 1804	i/5	
op.68	Symphony no.6 'Pastoral', F	1808; 22 Dec 1808	p: Leipzig, 1809	Prince Lobkowitz and Count Rasumovsky	i/6	
op.92	Symphony no.7, A	1811–12; 8 Dec 1813	s, p: Vienna, 1816	Count Moritz von Fries; arrs. for pf, pf 4 hands and 2 pf ded. Elisabeth Aleksiev, Empress of Russia	i/7	
op.93	Symphony no.8, F	1812; 27 Feb 1814	s, p: Vienna, 1817	shortened version of end of 1st movt, HS iv	i/8	
op.91	Wellingtons Sieg oder Die Schlacht bei Vittoria ('Battle Symphony')	1813; 8 Dec 1813	s, p: Vienna, 1816; for pf: London and Vienna, 1816	Prince Regent of England (later King George IV); orig. version of pt 2, for Maelzel's panharmonicon, HS iv	ii/10; HS viii [for pf]	ii/1
op.115	Overture 'Namensfeier', C	1814–15; 25 Dec 1815	s, p: Vienna, 1825	Prince Anton Heinrich Radziwill; incorporates ideas sketched several years earlier	iii/22	ii/1
woo3	Gratulations-Menuet, E♭	1822; 3 Nov 1822	p: Vienna, 1832	written for Carl Friedrich Hensler, ded. (by publisher) Karl Holz	ii/13	ii/3
op.125	Symphony no.9, d	1822–4; 7 May 1824	s, p: Mainz, 1826	Friedrich Wilhelm III of Prussia	i/9	

SOLO INSTRUMENTS AND ORCHESTRA

No.	Title, Key	Composition, First performance	Publication	Dedication, Remarks	GA	NA
woo4	Piano Concerto, E♭	1784	s: GA	survives only in pf score (with orch cues in solo part)	xxv/310	
Hess 13	Romance, e, pf, fl, bn, orch, frag.	?1786	Wiesbaden, 1952	intended as slow movt of larger work	HS iii	
woo5	Violin Concerto, C, frag.	1790–92	Vienna, 1879	part of 1st movt only; 1st edn ded. Gerhard von Breuning	HS iii	
Hess 12	Oboe Concerto, F, lost	?1792–3	—	sent to Bonn from Vienna in late 1793; a few sketches survive	—	—

Fig. 8.4 Extract from a *New Grove II* work-list for a major composer: Ludwig van Beethoven.

substantial entries on places (including towns and countries), non-musicians whose work has had a bearing on music, concepts, movements, methodologies, physical artefacts, institutions and a vast range of other categories.

Grove can be a starting and an ending point for reference or for programme-note or essay writing, but it can be only the beginning of a major research project. If you need to obtain facts and an authoritative overview on a subject, *Grove* is the best place to look. But if you are engaged in advanced research you may additionally need to use the work-lists and the writings cited in the bibliographies of *Grove* as the launching-pad for your project.

One of the problems that even practised researchers have found in using *Grove* is in determining the nature and the range of entries that might cast light on any given subject. Many of the most helpful articles – often very extensive ones – are under headings that do not readily spring to mind. This problem has been reduced by the publication of *New Grove II* on-line as well as in printed form, thus allowing not just a basic article search but also a full-text search. In other words, as well as being able to search for a specific article, you can find every occurrence of your chosen keyword throughout the dictionary. Volume 28 contains several invaluable bibliographical appendices, and Volume 29 has an index of the entire dictionary. Also, throughout *Grove* cross-references are given if another article has significant additional material about the subject of the entry you are reading.

Grove is available throughout the English-speaking world. Most people refer to it when they need to, but few study it to get a good understanding of how it works, so as to realize its full potential. An hour spent reading the introductory sections of *Grove* will help you get the maximum benefit from it. If you acquire the skill to navigate around the vast wealth of information contained in the twenty-nine volumes of *New Grove II*, you are on your way to being a methodical researcher.

Vincent Duckles's *Music Reference and Research Materials*

Duckles, Vincent H., and Ida Reed (eds), *Music Reference and Research Materials: An Annotated Bibliography*, 5th edn (New York: Schirmer Books, 1997).

Vincent Duckles was a librarian and musicologist based at the University of California at Berkeley. His single-volume guide to important research and reference materials was first published in 1964, and was aimed at postgraduate students and 'music reference librarians whose job it is to find the information they want'. The fifth edition of the book was published in 1997, and, like previous editions, it is an indispensable reference work. While *New Grove II* is the most comprehensive research tool, Duckles is an invaluable complement to it.

Duckles provides detailed bibliographical information about and brief evaluations of each work that is mentioned. It is selective rather than comprehensive (though it is more than 800 pages long), but the selection is extremely wide. The strength of Duckles lies not just in its scope, but also in the fact that it is easy to use. The references are arranged clearly under a number of subject headings and sub-headings, and there are many cross-references and indexes to help you find the information you are looking for (Fig. 8.5).

Basic reference books

Music reference books

This section is a very selective bibliography. It gives examples of some of the more helpful reference books that will serve as alternatives or additions to *New Grove II* or Duckles.

Baker, T., *Baker's Biographical Dictionary of Musicians*, revised by N. Slonimsky, 8th edn (New York: Schirmer Books, 1991).

A Bibliography of Discographies, 3 vols (New York: R. R. Bowker, 1977–83).

Brook, B. S., and R. Viano, *Thematic Catalogues in Music: An Annotated Bibliography*, 2nd edn (Stuyvesant, NY: Pendragon Press, 1997).

Brown, H. M., and S. Sadie, *Performance Practice*, New Grove Handbooks in Music/The Norton Grove Handbooks in Music, 2 vols (London: Macmillan; New York: W. W. Norton, 1990).

Caldwell, J., *Editing Early Music*, Early Music Series 5, 2nd edn (Oxford: Clarendon Press, 1985).

Campbell, M., and C. Greated, *The Musician's Guide to Acoustics* (London: J. M. Dent & Sons Ltd, 1987).

1.386   DICTIONARIES AND ENCYCLOPEDIAS

1.386 Ewen, David. *American Songwriters: An H.W. Wilson Biographical Dictionary.* 489 p
York: H.W. Wilson, 1987.

A successor to and total reorganization of his *Popular American Composers*, 1962, a
First Supplement, 1972.

A biographical dictionary covering 90 composers and 46 lyricists and composer–lyri
emphasizing biography over criticism and giving a brief history for 5,600 of the composers' so
which are indexed (pp. 453–89).

Reviewed by John E. Druesedow, Jr., in *ARBA* 19 (1988): no. 1267, with errata.

1.387* Gammond, Peter. *The Oxford Companion to Popular Music.* 739 pp. Oxford; New Yo
Oxford University Press, 1991.

Successor to the Gammond–Clayton *Guide to Popular Music* (London: Phoenix, 1960), 27
pp. Reprinted with corrections in 1993.

A dictionary of terms, musical instruments, concert halls, titles (song, album, show, and
film), and brief biographies, intended for both the student and the professional user in the many
international areas of popular music. There are indexes to people and groups (pp. 631–54,
shows and films (pp. 655–88), and songs and albums (pp. 689–739).

Reviewed by Amanda Maple in *Fontes* 40 (1993): 64–65.

1.388* Hale, Mark. *HeadBangers: The Worldwide Megabook of Heavy Metal Bands.* xxii + 542
pp. Ann Arbor, Mich.: Popular Culture, 1993. (PCI collector editions) (Rock & roll reference
series, 37)

An encyclopedia listing 3,458 heavy metal bands, with bibliographical and discographical
information from the 1960s to the 1980s. The preface discusses the subtleties of heavy metal
styles. The many helpful indexes include band names, performer names, bands and performers
(arranged by country), U.S. bands and performers (arranged by state), band styles and influ-

ing plates. Leipzig: Wolfga-
A facsimile reprint, edited by
(Documenta musicologica, I/3).

A landmark in the history of music reference
Lexicon established the pattern for modern dictionar-
such as Riemann (**1.45**) and Moser (**1.38**). It is also a primary source
baroque musical knowledge and practice, expanding Brossard's work (**1.**

1.60 Westrup, Jack, and Frank L. Harrison. *The New College Encyclopedia of Music.* Revise
Conrad Wilson. 608 pp. New York: W.W. Norton, 1976.

Published first in England as *Collins Music Encyclopedia*, 1959, and in the U.S. as the *New
College Encyclopedia of Music*, 1960, 739 pp. The present ed. was reprinted in Britain in 1984.
Encyclopedia of Music. The 1976 ed. was reprinted in the U.S. in 1981 and in Britain in 1984.

An encyclopedia less scholarly than informative. Its focus is on standard composers, terms,
and titles, with brief attention given to early and modern topics. There are severe summaries for
most important composers. There are occasional bibliographical references in the articles and
some illustrations, with musical quotations.

The 1960 ed. is reviewed by James B. Coover in *Notes* 17 (1960): 564–66.

1.61 Willemze, Theo. *Spectrum Muzieklexicon.* 4 vols. Utrecht: Het Spectrum, 1975.

A compendium of very brief entries, with composers, authors, and titles of pieces of music,
as well as definitions of terms. There are many cross-references from the major European
languages to Dutch, with extensive coverage of a broad span of Low Country musical culture. In
1981, the biographical entries were slightly updated and published separately in two volumes as
Componistenlexicon.

INTERNATIONAL BIOGRAPHY

In this section are dictionaries and encyclopedias, international in coverage, in which the emphasis is exclusively or mainly on people engaged in music-related activities, such as composers,
performers, scholars, critics, and impresarios. The line that separates biographical dictionaries
from volumes of collected biography is rather arbitrary. The distinction is essentially between
works that contain numerous brief entries

Fig. 8.5 Extracts from Duckles, showing part of the contents pages, the index and individual entries.

Clough, F. F., and G. J. Cuming, *The World's Encyclopedia of Recorded Music* (London: The London Gramophone Corp. in association with Sidgwick & Jackson, 1952). *First Supplement* (April 1950 to May–June 1951) is bound with the main volume; *Second Supplement* (1951–2) (London, 1952); *Third Supplement* (1953–5) (London, 1957; repr. by Greenwood Press, Westport, CT, 1970).

Gammond, P. (ed.), *The Oxford Companion to Popular Music* (Oxford University Press, 1991).

Hefele, B., *Jazz Bibliography: International Literature on Jazz, Blues, Spirituals, Gospel and Ragtime Music with a Selected List of Works on the Social and Cultural Background from the Beginning to the Present* (Munich; New York: K. G. Saur, 1981).

Hill, G. R., and N. L. Stephens, *Collected Historical Series and Sets and Monuments of Music* (Berkeley, CA: Fallen Leaf Press, 1997).

Hitchcock, H. W., and S. Sadie (eds), *The New Grove Dictionary of American Music*, 4 vols (New York: Grove's Dictionaries of Music; London: Macmillan, 1986).

Hoffmann, F. W., *The Literature of Rock, 1954–1978* (Metuchen, NJ: Scarecrow Press, 1981). Supplements: *The Literature of Rock II, 1979–1983*, with B. L. Cooper and L. A. Hoffmann, 2 vols (1986); *The Literature of Rock III, 1984–1990, with Additional Material for the Period 1954–1983*, with B. L. Cooper (1995).

Kernfeld, B. (ed.), *The New Grove Dictionary of Jazz*, 2 vols (London: Macmillan; New York: Grove's Dictionaries of Music, 1988; repr. in 1 volume, 1995).

Larkin, C. (ed.), *The Guinness Encyclopaedia of Popular Music*, 2nd edn, 6 vols (Enfield, Middlesex; New York: Guinness Publishers, Stockton Press, 1995).

Lawson, C., and R. Stowell, *The Historical Performance of Music: An Introduction* (Cambridge University Press, 1999).

The Music Index: A Subject-Author Guide to Current Music Periodical Literature (Detroit, MI: Information Service, Inc., Jan. 1949 onwards) (also available on CD-ROM).

Myers, H. (ed.), *The New Grove Handbook in Ethnomusicology*, 2 vols (London: Macmillan, 1993).

Nettl, B., *Reference Materials in Ethnomusicology: A Bibliographic Essay*, 2nd edn (Detroit, MI: Information Coordinators, 1967).

Randel, D. M. (ed.), *The New Harvard Dictionary of Music* (Cambridge, MA: Belknap Press; Harvard University Press, 1986).

—— , *The Harvard Biographical Dictionary of Music* (Cambridge, MA: Belknap Press; Harvard University Press, 1996).

RILM Abstracts of Music Literature, Répertoire international de littérature musicale / International Repertory of Music Literature / Internationales Repertorium der Musikliteratur (New York: International *RILM* Center, 1967–), Vol. 1– (available on CD-ROM and on-line).

Sadie, J. A., and R. Samuel (eds), *The New Grove Dictionary of Women Composers* (London: Macmillan, 1994); American edn, *The Norton/Grove Dictionary of Women Composers* (New York: W. W. Norton).

Sadie, S. (ed.), *The New Grove Dictionary of Musical Instruments*, 3 vols (London: Macmillan Press; New York: Grove's Dictionaries of Music, 1984).

——, and C. Bashford (eds), *The New Grove Dictionary of Opera*, 4 vols (London: Macmillan; New York: Grove's Dictionaries of Music, 1992).

Shepherd, J., and D. Horn, D. Laing, P. Oliver, P. Tagg and J. Wilson (eds and compilers), *Popular Music Studies: A Select International Bibliography* (London: Mansell, 1997).

Other reference books

Drabble, M. (ed.), *The Oxford Companion to English Literature*, 6th edn (Oxford University Press, 1995).

Encyclopaedia Britannica, 32 vols, 15th edn (Chicago: Encyclopaedia Britannica, Inc., 1985) (available on CD-ROM and on-line as *Britannica Online*).

Evans, H., and M. Evans (compilers), *Picture Researcher's Handbook: An International Guide to Picture Sources and How to Use Them*, 6th edn (London: Routledge, 1996).

Mitchell, B. R. (ed.), *International Historical Statistics: Africa, Asia and Oceania 1750–1993; The Americas 1750–1993; Europe 1750–1993*, 3 vols, 3rd edn (London: Macmillan, 1998).

Simpson, J. A., and E. S. C. Weiner (eds), *The Oxford English Dictionary*, 2nd edn (Oxford: Clarendon Press, 1989) (available on-line).

Stephen, L., and S. Lee (eds), *Dictionary of National Biography*, 22 vols (London: Smith Elder, 1908–09); supplements published every 5 or 10 years until 1990 by Oxford University Press [*New Dictionary of National Biography* due for publication by Oxford University Press in 2004].

Turner, J., (ed.), *The Dictionary of Art*, 34 vols (London: Macmillan; New York: Grove's Dictionaries, 1996) (available on-line as *The Grove Dictionary of Art*).

Writers' and Artists' Yearbook (London: A. & C. Black [published annually]).

World Wide Web sites

Web sites can be helpful to music researchers in two respects: they provide information in their own right and they can also link you to other sites where you can find the information you are looking for. The list given below includes sites from both categories. Most of the sites listed are free, but some (sometimes called password-protected sites) may only be available on subscription. However, many password-protected sites are available through computers in college or public libraries.

I have given priority to music 'meta-sites' or portals. These are sites that do not simply provide information about the services and facilities offered by an organization or institution; they also give links to many other relevant sites worldwide.

You should explore these sites to find the ones that are reliable and most useful to you. Keep a collection of 'bookmarks' (or 'favourites'). But be selective; always evaluate the sites and compare them with each other. I should emphazise that it is important for you not to rely entirely on Web sites for information. You will see that the best sites regularly direct their readers to printed books. This is the best way to use these sites. Use them as a tool for finding things; do not rely on the Web to provide you with all the detailed information you are looking for.

Some sites have an interactive facility: for example, The British Library site allows you to search its catalogues. You should remember (as I pointed out earlier) the difference between the American and English spelling of some words when using these search facilities, and also remember not to type characters that look similar but are entirely different as far as the computer is concerned (such as the letters O and I and the figures 0 and 1).

The USA exercises an enormous influence on the World Wide Web, and this is hardly surprising given its prominence in developing Internet facilities. You should also be aware how quickly the content of the World Wide Web is changing. You will encounter messages such as 'Site under construction' and other messages in which the word 'ERROR' is prominent. This usually means that a site has been withdrawn but the link to it still remains in place. Do not worry about this; it merely goes to illustrate the difference between the World Wide Web and more traditional methods of communication.

The list of music sites below is followed by a list of other useful sites. You will find that many of the sites mentioned here are linked to each other. The *Music in Words* Web page <http://www.abrsmpub lishing.co.uk/musicinwords> has links to all sites mentioned in this book. It is regularly updated with relevant new sites.

Music sites

Associated Board of the Royal Schools of Music (ABRSM's own site):
    <http://www.abrsm.org>
BBC Education site (includes keyword search facilities for music education):
    <http://www.bbc.co.uk/education>
Classical Search (widely based, commercially sponsored portal for music):
    <http://www.classicalsearch.com>
Doctoral Dissertations in Musicology – Online (run by Indiana University Music School):
    <http://www.music.indiana.edu/ddm/>
Indiana University Bloomington Libraries: William and Gayle Cook Music Library (the front-running university music Web site in the USA, wide-ranging with an impressive collection of links):
    <http://www.music.indiana.edu/musicref/>
International Association of Music Information Centres (gives links to the sites of music information centres in most countries):
    <http://www.iamic.ie/>
New York Public Library for the Performing Arts: Selected Music Resources on the Internet (a well-organized American public library site with good links):
    <http://www.nypl.org/research/lpa/mus/mus.resources.html>

The Open University (the UK's largest university and the biggest distance-teaching institution in the world):
<http://www.open.ac.uk/Arts/music/>

PALATINE (Performing Arts Learning and Teaching Innovation Network) (the UK universities' focus for on-line music facilities):
<http://www.lancs.ac.uk/users/palatine/>

RIPM (*Répertoire international de la presse musicale* – on-line information about indexes of earlier music-periodical literature):
<http://www.nisc.com/ripm/>

Royal Holloway College, University of London, The Golden Pages: Links for Musicians on the WWW (one of the best UK sites – also includes an archive of music PhD abstracts):
<http://www.sun.rhbnc.ac.uk/Music/Links/index.html>

Shrine to Music: University of South Dakota (one of the largest museums of musical instruments in the world):
<http://www.usd.edu/smm/>

Sibelius Academy: Music Resources (excellent Finland-based site):
<http://www.siba.fi/Kulttuuripalvelut/music.html>

Bibliographical sites

The British Library (allows you to access and search the music catalogues of The British Library, as well as all its other catalogues):
<http://www.bl.uk/>
(Go to 'Collections', then 'Music'.)

General encyclopedias, dictionaries and other reference sites

Britannica Online (*Encyclopaedia Britannica* in its on-line form – comprehensive and with many links):
<http://britannica.com>

Cartography Department of the University of Utrecht in the Netherlands (a huge, impressively organized and apparently comprehensive collection of maps):
<http://oddens.geog.uu.nl>

CIA Factbook (contemporary statistical information with maps on every country in the world):
<http://www.odci.gov/cia/publications/factbook/>

The Library of Congress (USA) (sophisticated and extremely useful site that includes many sound recordings, photographs and sheet music held by the library):
<http://www.loc.gov/>

Oxford English Dictionary (the best dictionary, but password-protected; worth looking at for its explanation of how it works):
<http://oed.com/public/guide>

Refdesk.com (includes links to several free on-line dictionaries and encyclopedias):
<http://www.refdesk.com>

On-line Internet tutorials

BBC Education Webwise site:
<http://www.bbc.co.uk/webwise/>

Evaluating Information Found on the Internet:
<http://milton.mse.jhu.edu/research/education/net.html>

Finding Information on the Internet: A TUTORIAL (UC Berkeley):
<http://www.lib.berkeley.edu/TeachingLib/Guides/Internet/>

TONIC: Interactive Netskills (excellent on-line tutorial course from the University of Newcastle, UK):
<http://www.netskills.ac.uk/TonicNG/cgi/sesame?tng>

Chapter nine

CITATIONS I: THE PRINTED WORD

THE INFORMATION given here assumes that you have read and understood the explanation of bibliographies and basic citation conventions given in Chapter 4. By necessity, there is a great deal of detail in this chapter. This is because, as with Chapters 10 and 11, it is designed to stand as a reference list for how to cite sources. These citation formalities are necessary in scholarly writing, but some of the information given here might be helpful to forms of writing for which such rules are not required. The details contained here will also be helpful for research, because they will enable you to understand the way information is presented in scholarly books.

The layout of this part of the book is very straightforward. I have listed and illustrated all the main types of printed source that you are likely to need to cite, in most cases according to the conventions of both the short-title and the author–date systems (in that order). However, there are some instances where the differences between these two systems need not apply (see 'Dictionary and encyclopedia entries', for instance), so in these cases I have chosen instead to give a simple citation method which will be appropriate whether your main citation method is the short-title or the author-date system. I have also given any additional or special information that is relevant. If you have difficulty in finding what you are looking for, you should refer to the index at the back of the book.

Under 'Books (individual)', meaning books that are not part of a series or multi-volume set, I have again covered the citation conventions that are explained in Chapter 4. This is the basic 'formula' for book citations. Additional factors that arise – for example, when a book has more than one author or publisher, or is a new edition of an earlier publication – are dealt with under their own headings. In the entries on 'Academic journals' and 'Books (individual)' I have also reminded you of the patterns for foot- and endnotes and in-text references, but I have not referred again to these in the later entries, unless there is some special point to note in a particular case. If you are unsure about notes and in-text references, turn back to Chapter 4 and the section on 'How to cite sources in text: as footnotes, endnotes or in-text references?'.

Academic journals

Academic journals are scholarly publications. They are 'periodicals' that are generally published every few months or once a year. Usually:
- there is a new *volume* of the journal every year;
- that volume is made up of several *issues.*

For example, Volume 27 of the journal *Early Music* was published in 1999, and this was made up of four issues, published in February, May, August and November. The volume number of a journal is usually given in arabic numbers, even if the journal itself uses roman numbers (as *Early Music* does, in fact). There is no need to use the word 'volume' or the abbreviation 'vol.'. The issue number is also given in arabic, and is separated from the volume number by a colon.

In your bibliography you should normally cite the specific articles you have consulted rather than simply citing the journal. It is important to remember that whenever you cite a journal article, it is the name of the *journal* that is italicized, *not* the title of the article. This is because, for bibliographical purposes, it is the journal that is the publication – the articles are just part of it. In the short-title system the *article* title is given in quotation marks, but in the author–date system it is given without them.

The example below is an article from *Early Music* 27:1 (Volume 27, Issue 1). When citing journal articles, bear in mind that:
- the full bibliographical reference must include the numbers of the first and last pages of the article (here, pages 96 to 118);
- in citing the titles of journal articles, many publishers capitalize only the initial letter of the first word and any proper nouns (names, places etc.);
- the abbreviations 'p.' and 'pp.' for 'page' and 'pages' are commonly left out.

SHORT-TITLE SYSTEM

This is how you would cite the article in your bibliography:

Page, J. K., 'Music and the royal procession in Maria Theresia's Vienna',
    Early Music, 27:1 (1999), 96–118.

If you wish to quote some material from, for example, page 100 of
the article, the citation will look almost identical to the bibliographical reference above. The one key difference is that you need to cite
the *specific* page number, '100', which would replace the page-range
numbers given in the bibliography. Remember also that, in contrast
to their order in the bibliography, here the author's initials come
before the surname:

J. K. Page, 'Music and the royal procession in Maria Theresia's Vienna',
    Early Music, 27:1 (1999), 100.

For subsequent quotations or references to the article, you do not
need to give the full bibliographical details, but simply the author
surname, a shortened version of the article title and the specific page
number(s). There is no need to give the details of the journal itself in
the shortened version of the reference, as these will be easily found in
the bibliography, if you have first cited the article in the form given
above. For example:

Page, 'Music and the royal procession', 113.

AUTHOR–DATE SYSTEM

Below is the bibliographical citation in the author–date style; the
information is identical, but the format and punctuation are
different:

Page, J. K. 1999. Music and the royal procession in Maria Theresia's
    Vienna. *Early Music*, 27:1, 96–118.

For an in-text reference, the information will simply refer to the
author's surname and date, and to any page reference. Again, there is
no need to give the details of the journal itself in the in-text reference,
as these will be found in the bibliography. If you were referring to a
quotation you had taken from, for example, page 100 of the article,
the in-text reference would be placed immediately after the quotation, and would take the following form:

(Page 1999, 100)

All further references would follow the same basic pattern of author
surname and publication date, separated by a comma from the page
number, and all enclosed in brackets.

Advertisements and posters

Advertisements (such as advertisements for the sale of musical instruments) printed in newspapers should be cited using the convention explained below under 'Newspapers and magazines'. Advertising and other posters that you have found in a museum or other archive should be cited using the convention explained in Chapter 11 under 'Museum exhibits and other archived objects'.

Books (individual)

By 'book', I mean any one-off publication that is not a part of a series such as a multi-volume series, a newspaper or an academic journal.

SHORT-TITLE SYSTEM

> Ehrlich, C., *First Philharmonic: A History of the Royal Philharmonic Society* (Oxford: Clarendon Press, 1995).

In contrast to the practice with journal articles (see above), publishers commonly capitalize the initial letter of every major word in a book title. (Words like 'and' and 'the' do not count as major words, so would only take an initial capital if they were the first word of the title or subtitle.) Also, the abbreviations 'p.' and 'pp.' ('page'/'pages') are used.

If you wish to quote from or refer to a point found on, for example, page 75 of Ehrlich's book, the first reference will be given thus:

> C. Ehrlich, *First Philharmonic: A History of the Royal Philharmonic Society* (Oxford: Clarendon Press, 1995), p. 75.

(Note that the author's initials come before the surname, in contrast to the order in the bibliographical citation.) Subsequent references (for example, to page 84) will look like this:

> Ehrlich, *First Philharmonic*, p. 84.

AUTHOR–DATE SYSTEM

> Ehrlich, C. 1995. *First Philharmonic: A History of the Royal Philharmonic Society*. Oxford: Clarendon Press.

An in-text reference (for example, to page 75) will look like this:

> (Ehrlich 1995, 75)

Books published in more than one place

Many publishers are based in more than one country. If a publisher has published a book in more than one of the cities where it has head-quarters, the title page will list each of the cities. When you cite a book with two or more places of publication, you should separate each place name with a semicolon, then put a colon followed by the name of the publisher.

SHORT-TITLE SYSTEM

> Hindle Hazen, M., and R. Hazen, *The Music Men: An Illustrated History of Brass Bands in America, 1800–1920* (Washington, D.C.; London: Smithsonian Press, 1987).

AUTHOR–DATE SYSTEM

> Hindle Hazen, M., and R. Hazen. 1987. *The Music Men: An Illustrated History of Brass Bands in America, 1800–1920.* Washington, DC; London: Smithsonian Press.

(See also 'Books with more than one publisher' below.)

Books that are part of a multi-volume series or set

A work may be published in more than one volume for several reasons – perhaps because it is simply too long for one volume, or because it is part of a series published at intervals (for instance, annually, as with a yearbook).

Many institutions and organizations publish yearbooks. In 1980 the British Museum published its fourth yearbook, and on this occasion it was devoted to music. Where a serial publication such as this is concerned, in addition to the title and publication details of the specific book, you also need to give the series title and number, which should follow the book title. To distinguish it from the book title, the series title should not be italicized.

SHORT-TITLE SYSTEM

> Mitchell, T. C. (ed.), *Music and Civilisation,* British Museum Yearbook 4 (London: British Museum Publications Ltd, 1980).

For a single work that is published in more than one volume, you need to indicate in the bibliography how many volumes there are.

This information is placed after the book title and before the bracket containing the publication details:

Scholes, P., *The Mirror of Music 1844–1944: A Century of Musical Life in Britain as Reflected in the Pages of the Musical Times*, 2 vols (London: Novello & Co. Ltd, 1947).

AUTHOR–DATE SYSTEM

Mitchell, T. C. (ed.). 1980. *Music and Civilisation*. British Museum Yearbook 4. London: British Museum Publications Ltd.

Scholes, P. 1947. *The Mirror of Music 1844–1944: A Century of Musical Life in Britain as Reflected in the Pages of the Musical Times*. 2 vols. London: Novello & Co. Ltd.

Books with more than one author or editor

If a book is written or edited by more than one person, the author or editor whose name is given first on the book should also come first in the bibliographical reference. That name will be inverted (the surname appears first, followed by the initial or full first name), but the other authors' or editors' names need not be inverted. (Whether you invert the other names or not is up to you, but be consistent in whatever you decide.)

Also, be consistent in your use of either the symbol '&' (ampersand) or the word 'and' between the authors' or editors' names.

SHORT-TITLE SYSTEM

Keyte, H., and A. Parrott (eds), *The New Oxford Book of Carols* (Oxford University Press, 1992).

AUTHOR–DATE SYSTEM

Keyte, H., and A. Parrott (eds). 1992. *The New Oxford Book of Carols*. Oxford University Press.

Books with more than one publisher

Many books are jointly published (co-published) by two or more publishers. With such books, you need to give the details of each publisher, separated by a semicolon. The following example is a book jointly published by the Royal National Theatre and Nick Hern

Books to coincide with the British premiere of the musical *Sunday in the Park with George* by Stephen Sondheim and his collaborator James Lapine. The order in which the publishers are given will depend on the order in which their names appear in the book itself.

SHORT-TITLE SYSTEM

> Sondheim, S., and J. Lapine, *Sunday in the Park with George* (London: Royal National Theatre; Nick Hern Books, 1986).

AUTHOR–DATE SYSTEM

> Sondheim, S., and J. Lapine. 1986. *Sunday in the Park with George.* London: Royal National Theatre; Nick Hern Books.

Chapters or essays in books

You may find that you need to cite a specific chapter or essay in a book, particularly where the chapters or essays are written by different authors (a multi-authored work). The conventions are very similar to those for journal articles (although here you also have a volume editor to consider). In particular, you should give the numbers of the first and last pages of the chapter. The details of the chapter should come first, followed by the details of the book. While the title of the *book* is always given in italics, in the short-title system the *chapter* title is given in quotation marks, but in the author–date system it is given without them.

If your reader is to locate the chapter easily in the bibliography, it is best to list it under the chapter author's name and the chapter title (as below), rather than under the volume editor's name and the book title. However, if you think the book is important as a whole, you should include it in the bibliography in its own right, under the volume editor's name.

SHORT-TITLE SYSTEM

> Bythell, D., 'The brass band in the Antipodes: the transplantation of British popular culture', in T. Herbert (ed.), *The British Brass Band: A Musical and Social History* (Oxford University Press, 2000), pp. 217–44.

> Bythell, D. 2000. The brass band in the Antipodes: the transplantation of British popular culture. In *The British Brass Band: A Musical and Social History*, ed. T. Herbert, pp. 217–44. Oxford University Press.

Conference papers (published and unpublished)

Many publications arise from academic conferences. Academics meet and read papers about the findings of their research. These papers are then published in the 'proceedings' of the conference.

For papers published in the proceedings of a conference, follow the conventions explained above in 'Chapters or essays in books'.

In addition to the author and title of the paper, references to *unpublished* conference papers should include the name of the conference's organizing body and the title, place and date of the conference. In the short-title system the title is given in quotation marks; in the author–date system it is given without them.

SHORT-TITLE SYSTEM

> Benson, S., 'The piano as a domestic status symbol in the early 20th century', paper presented at the Cultural Musicology Society Congress, London, 1–5 November 2000.

AUTHOR–DATE SYSTEM

> Benson, S. 2000. The piano as a domestic status symbol in the early 20th century. Paper presented at the Cultural Musicology Society Congress, London, 1–5 November.

Dictionary and encyclopedia entries

References to entries in dictionaries or encyclopedias look somewhat different from references to other kinds of published books. For one thing, it is usually taken to be unnecessary, provided that the dictionary in question is well known, to provide the publication details; for another, page and volume numbers are not normally cited. Rather, the abbreviation 's.v.' (*sub verbo*, meaning 'under the word' or 'see under') is followed by the name of the entry in quotes. So, for instance, a reference to the entry on 'New Orleans' in *New Grove II* (see Chapter 8) would be given either in end- or footnotes, or in brackets as an in-text reference, and would look like this:

New Grove II, s.v. 'New Orleans'.

(If the edition of the dictionary you have used is not the first edition, you must specify which edition you have consulted.)

The current editions of well-known reference works such as *Grove* are not normally included in a bibliography, but early editions of such works (for example, the first edition of *Grove*) should be included because they could have the status of a primary source.

Dissertations and theses

Most dissertations and theses are unpublished, so they need a special citation method. The title should be given in roman, not italics, and the degree that it earned (PhD, MA, MMus and so on) and the university should be specified. In the short-title system the title is given in quotation marks; in the author–date system it is given without them.

SHORT-TITLE SYSTEM

> Jones, J. B., 'The piano and chamber works of Gabriel Fauré' (PhD dissertation, Cambridge University, 1974).

AUTHOR–DATE SYSTEM

> Jones, J. B. 1974. The piano and chamber works of Gabriel Fauré. PhD dissertation. Cambridge University.

If a dissertation or thesis is published, it should be cited as a book.

Edited works

An editor prepares and organizes other people's texts for publication or performance. These texts may take a variety of forms: a volume of scholarly essays by several contributors, a novel or diary by a single writer, the letters exchanged between two or more people, or a musical work, for example. Where the work is a collection of scholarly essays, the editor(s) takes the place of an author in the bibliographical citation, but with the abbreviation '(ed.)' or '(eds)' after the name(s).

Where the edition is of the work of a single author or composer who is named, as in the Mozart example below, the author's name should come first, and the editor's name should be given after the title, preceded by the abbreviation 'ed.' or 'eds' (without brackets).

> Leyshon, A., D. Matless and G. Revill (eds), *The Place of Music* (New York; London: Guilford Press, 1998).

> Mozart, W. A., *Symphony in G Minor*, K. 550, ed. N. Broder (New York: W. W. Norton, 1967).

AUTHOR–DATE SYSTEM

> Leyshon, A., D. Matless and G. Revill (eds). 1998. *The Place of Music*. New York; London: Guilford Press.

> Mozart, W. A. 1967. *Symphony in G Minor*, K. 550. Ed. N. Broder. New York: W. W. Norton.

(See also 'New editions' below.)

Facsimiles and other reproductions

A facsimile is a photographic reproduction of an earlier work. It is therefore an unrevised reprint (see also 'Reprints' below). The citation for such works needs to accommodate not just the details of the facsimile, but also those of the original work. The abbreviation 'repr.' (reprinted) identifies the new version from the original, and should be followed by any additional information about the new publication (such as the inclusion of an introductory essay, as in the following example).

SHORT-TITLE SYSTEM

> Rose, A., *Talks with Bandsmen: A Popular Handbook for Brass Instrumentalists* (London: William Rider, 1895; repr. with an introduction by Arnold Myers, London: Tony Bingham, 1995).

AUTHOR–DATE SYSTEM

> Rose, A. 1995. *Talks with Bandsmen: A Popular Handbook for Brass Instrumentalists*. London: William Rider, 1895; repr. with an introduction by Arnold Myers, London: Tony Bingham.

Journals

See 'Academic journals' above.

Letters

For how to cite your own personal correspondence, see Chapter 11, 'Personal communications'. For unpublished correspondence between third parties, see Chapter 11, 'Unpublished manuscripts in libraries and archives'. For published correspondence, you should find the advice you need in the entries on books, journals and chapters or essays.

New editions

A new edition of a book is one in which the original text has been changed or added to significantly (as opposed to a reprint – see 'Reprints' below). A new edition may be referred to by number (2nd edn, 3rd edn and so on), or it may be called a 'revised edition' (rev. edn). There is no need to specify the edition number if you are referring to the first edition, but you will need to do so for any further edition.

SHORT-TITLE SYSTEM

Baldauf-Berges, J. L., *Women Musicians of Venice: Musical Foundations, 1525–1855*, rev. edn (Oxford: Clarendon Press, 1996).

Russell, D., *Popular Music in England, 1840–1914*, 2nd edn (Manchester; New York: Manchester University Press, 1997).

AUTHOR–DATE SYSTEM

Baldauf-Berges, J. L. 1996. *Women Musicians of Venice: Musical Foundations, 1525–1855.* Rev. edn. Oxford: Clarendon Press.

Russell, D. 1997. *Popular Music in England, 1840–1914.* 2nd edn. Manchester; New York: Manchester University Press.

Newspapers and magazines

Some newspaper articles carry the name of the author, others do not. It is important that you cite all the relevant information you can obtain about a source. It is especially important that you cite the proper title of the publication (not its abbreviated or local title), because many countries publish newspapers with similar titles – for instance, *The Times* and the *New York Times*. If there is a danger of confusion, give the country of publication in brackets after the title. ('The' is usually omitted from newspaper and magazine titles, except for publications with one-word titles, for example *The Times* and *The Economist.*)

Unless you think it is particularly important to do so, it is not necessary to list newspaper and magazine articles in your bibliography. It is usually enough to give the title and date of the paper in a foot- or endnote, or in brackets after the quotation or reference.

Page references are not normally given for a daily newspaper, as it may have several different editions, and the position of an article may differ from edition to edition. However, with a weekly or monthly newspaper or magazine, it is appropriate to give page references.

Novels

If you refer to a novel only occasionally, there is no need to include it in your bibliography and notes. It is, however, good practice not only to mention the title and the author, but also to give the date when the novel was originally published. For example:

In *Great Expectations* (1860–1) Dickens draws on similar themes…

If, however, you quote from the novel or make substantial reference to it, the bibliography should contain the details of the precise edition of the novel you used. If the edition is part of a well-known series such as Penguin Classics, the series title and the date of that particular edition are sufficient, though the original date of publication may be given in a square bracket after the title.

If the edition is less well-known, the name of the editor and the full publication details should be given, as explained in 'Edited works' above.

Any quotations or specific references should be accompanied by end- or footnotes in the usual manner.

SHORT-TITLE SYSTEM

Dickens, C., *Great Expectations*, [1860–1], Penguin Classics (1986).

AUTHOR–DATE SYSTEM

Dickens, C. 1986. *Great Expectations*. [1860–1]. Penguin Classics.

Official and government documents

Official and government documents include such items as laws and statutes, reports of government committees and the debates that take place in the legislature of a country. *The Chicago Manual of Style* (see bibliography at the end of this chapter) provides detailed advice on American, Canadian and British government and public documents. There is no standard pattern for the citation of official documents; the information you are able to give will depend on what is supplied by the official body that issued the document. If there is a possibility of confusion, you give the name of the country concerned as the first part of the citation. Official documents do not usually have a named author, so the citation should give the name of the body or agency that issued the document, the title of the document in italics and the publication date. There may also be a series or publication number, and page and column references. For instance, the following citation refers to the proceedings of a British governmental committee, meeting in 1892 to investigate the use of theatres and music halls.

SHORT-TITLE SYSTEM

> United Kingdom, House of Commons, *Parliamentary Papers*, 1892, Select Committee on Theatres and Places of Entertainment, XVIII, 240, cols 3004–6.

AUTHOR–DATE SYSTEM

> United Kingdom. House of Commons. 1892. *Parliamentary Papers*. Select Committee on Theatres and Places of Entertainment. XVIII, 240, cols 3004–6.

Periodicals

See 'Academic journals' and 'Newspapers and magazines' above.

Plays

The following advice may be appropriate not only in respect of plays, but also of librettos. Plays are usually organized into acts and scenes, and the dialogue may also be numbered by line. If you quote from a play, a common practice is to refer to the act in roman numbering, followed by the number of the scene in arabic numbering and, if relevant, the line numbers (also in arabic). Page numbers are only necessary where line numbers are not used. This kind of reference is so succinct that it can be given in brackets after the quotation, rather than in an end- or footnote.

For example, if you wanted to quote lines 20–25 from Act IV, Scene 3 of Shakespeare's Hamlet, your reference after the quotation would look like this:

(*Hamlet*, IV.3. 20–25)

The title of the play can be omitted from such a reference if you have already named it and are clearly still discussing that particular play.

When you give the title of a play, it should be in italics. It is also good practice to give the date of the play in brackets after the title. If discussion of the play forms a substantial part of your argument, you should give the publication details of the edition you have used in your bibliography. The date of the original publication may be given in square brackets after the title.

SHORT-TITLE SYSTEM

Sartre, J.-P., *Crime passionnel*, [1949], trans. K. Black (London: Methuen, 1996).

('Trans.' means 'translated by' or 'translator' – see 'Translations' below.)

AUTHOR–DATE SYSTEM

Sartre, J.-P. 1996. *Crime passionnel*. [1949]. Trans. K. Black. London: Methuen.

Poems

The following advice may be appropriate in respect of poems set to music. Like plays, poems (and particularly long poems) are often numbered line by line. If a poem has line numbers, you should give the relevant numbers. The same applies if the poem is divided into books. This kind of reference is so succinct that it need not be given in an end- or footnote, but may be placed in brackets after the quotation. For example, if you wanted to quote the first two lines of Book IV of *Paradise Lost*, your reference would look like this:

(*Paradise Lost*, IV. 1–2)

The title of the poem can be left out of such a reference if you have already named the poem and are clearly still discussing it.

When you give the title of a short poem, it should be in quotation marks. The titles of long poems – that is, poems that form a complete book or several books, such as Homer's *Iliad*, or Milton's *Paradise Lost* – should be given in italics. It is good practice to give the date of the poem in brackets after the title, but unless you have quoted more than a few words from it, there is no need to give the details of the publication in which it appears. If, however, the discussion of the poem is particularly important to your argument, then the publication details of the edition or collection you have used should be given. The poem may be in a collection of a single poet's work, or in an anthology put together by an editor. In either case, the usual conventions for authored or edited works apply.

SHORT-TITLE SYSTEM

> Thomas, R. S., *Later Poems 1972–1982* (London: Macmillan, 1983).

> Wain, J. (ed.), *The Oxford Anthology of English Poetry: Spenser to Crabbe* (Oxford University Press, 1990).

AUTHOR–DATE SYSTEM

> Thomas, R. S. 1983. *Later Poems 1972–1982*. London: Macmillan.

> Wain, J. (ed.). 1990. *The Oxford Anthology of English Poetry: Spenser to Crabbe*. Oxford University Press.

Religious writings

While titles of published books are normally given in italics, titles of sacred and revered texts are normally given in roman, without quotes. For instance:

Bhagavad Gita	Bible	Hebrew Bible
New English Bible	Qur'an	Talmud

Similarly for parts of such books, special prayers and so on:

Genesis	Kaddish	Magnificat	Old Testament
Te Deum	Ten Commandments		

As with dictionaries and encyclopedias, unless you feel that it is important that you direct your readers to a particular edition of the work in question, there is no need to cite works such as these in your list of references or bibliography. There is no need to use foot- or endnotes; it is sufficient to give the title of the book, and the chapter and verse or line number in brackets after a quotation or direct reference. For example, if you wanted to refer your reader to verse 17 in Chapter 7 of the book of Revelation, one of the books of the New Testament, your reference would read:

(Revelation 7.17)

You should consider whether it is necessary to mention the version or edition of the text you quote from, but there is no need to mention the Old or New Testament or the Bible by name when citing a book of the Bible in a reference.

Reprints

Reprinting a book does not mean publishing a new edition, but simply printing further copies with perhaps a few minor corrections (typing errors and so on) that have been spotted in the previous print-run. The date of the reprint (indicated by the abbreviation 'repr.') should be given in addition to the publication date.

SHORT-TITLE SYSTEM

Broughton, S., M. Ellingham, D. Muddyman and R. Trillo, *World Music: The Rough Guide* (London: Rough Guides Ltd, 1994; repr. 1995).

AUTHOR–DATE SYSTEM

Broughton, S., M. Ellingham, D. Muddyman and R. Trillo. 1995. *World Music: The Rough Guide*. 1994. Repr. London: Rough Guides Ltd.

(See also 'Facsimiles and other reproductions' above for unrevised reprints.)

Translations

In citing a work that has been translated from one language into another, you need to give the names of both the original writer and the translator (identified by the abbreviation 'trans.'). If the original writer is named as the author, then the work should be listed in the bibliography under his or her surname. If the original writer's name forms part of the title, as in the second example below, then the work should be listed under the name of the translator (who may also be the editor).

SHORT-TITLE SYSTEM

> Berlioz, H., *A Treatise on Modern Instrumentation and Orchestration*, trans. M. C. Clarke, 2nd edn (London: Novello, Ewer & Co., 1858).

> Cairns, D. (trans. and ed.), *The Memoirs of Hector Berlioz* (London: Gollancz, 1977).

AUTHOR–DATE SYSTEM

> Berlioz, H. 1858. *A Treatise on Modern Instrumentation and Orchestration*. Trans. M. C. Clarke. 2nd edn. London: Novello, Ewer & Co.

> Cairns, D. (trans. and ed.). 1977. *The Memoirs of Hector Berlioz*. London: Gollancz.

Bibliography

Butcher, J., *Copy-Editing: The Cambridge Handbook for Editors, Authors and Publishers*, 3rd edn (Cambridge University Press, 1992).

The Chicago Manual of Style, 14th edn (University of Chicago Press, 1993).

Gibaldi, J., *MLA Handbook for Writers of Research Papers*, 4th edn (New York: The Modern Language Association of America, 1995).

Hart's Rules for Compositors and Readers at the University Press, Oxford, 39th edn (Oxford University Press, 1983).

MHRA Style Book, 5th edn (London: The Modern Humanities Research Association, 1996).

Chapter ten

CITATIONS II: MUSICAL SOURCES

T HIS CHAPTER is devoted to citation conventions for musical works, performances and other items specific to music. The distinction between the author–date and short-title systems (see Chapters 4 and 9) is much less important here, because they don't usually apply; it is only with complete editions and published scores that you would need to take a decision as to which system to use (see 'Complete editions of a composer's works' and 'Published scores' below). As I have said before, there is hardly ever just one definitive way of citing a particular source, but as far as musical sources are concerned, in most instances the differences between approaches are so slight that in the interests of clarity and simplicity I have chosen to follow just one method. One of the main points to note is the use of punctuation marks and italics.

Ballets

See under 'Music compositions' below.

CDs, records and other recordings

Recordings should be listed not in your bibliography, but rather in a separate discography, which serves the same purpose – to provide all the necessary details of the recordings you have used, so that your reader can trace them if necessary. Where the recording is either entirely or primarily of works by a single composer, the parts of the reference should be given in the following order:

- the composer's name;
- the title of the disc (probably in italics, but if the title of the disc is the same as the name of the musical piece or pieces played in the recording, you should consult the guidelines given below under 'Music compositions' as to whether to use italics or not);

- the name of the performer(s);
- the date of copyright or publication (the date preceded by the symbol © or ℗ on the record sleeve or CD liner);
- the type of recording (CD, audiocassette, vinyl record, wax cylinder, for example);
- if it is a set, the number of discs or cassettes in the set;
- the name of the record company;
- the catalogue number of the recording (this is given on the label).

Full stops are the clearest way to separate the different items of information:

> Palestrina. Mass *Hodie Christus Natus Est.* Gabrieli Consort and Players, Paul McCreesh. 1993. Compact disc. Archiv Produktion. 437 833–2.

If the recording is a compilation of pieces by various people, or if the works are anonymous, the title of the disc is given first, in italics:

> *20 Gramophone All-Time Greats.* Various artists. 1993. Compact disc. ASV. CD AJA 5112.

However, if the collection is performed by a well-known performer, the citation may start with the performer's name:

> Louis Armstrong. *The 25 Greatest Hot Fives and Hot Sevens.* 1995. Compact disc. ASV. CD AJA 5171.

CD sleeve/liner notes

These may not necessarily have a named author, but give the name first where there is one. You should then give the full recording information as set out above in 'CDs, records and other recordings':

> Al Hilgart, liner note to *Ella Fitzgerald sings the Rodgers and Hart Song Book.* 1997. Compact disc. Verve. 537 258–2.

If the author of the liner note is not named, the reference will simply read:

> Liner note to *Ella Fitzgerald sings the Rodgers and Hart Song Book.* 1997. Compact disc. Verve. 537 258–2.

Chamber music

See under 'Music compositions' below.

Choreographed dances

See under 'Music compositions: Ballets and other choreographed dances' below.

Complete editions of a composer's works

The complete works of several major composers have been published in scholarly editions. These are always multi-volume sets, so it is essential that the edition and the volume number are given. The format of the citation will depend on whether you are using the short-title or author–date system (see Chapters 4 and 9).

SHORT-TITLE SYSTEM

> Schmid, E. F., W. Plath and W. Rehm (eds), *W. A. Mozart: Neue Ausgabe sämtlicher Werke*, Internationale Stiftung Mozarteum Salzburg (Kassel: Bärenreiter, 1955–).

AUTHOR–DATE SYSTEM

> Schmid, E. F., W. Plath and W. Rehm (eds). 1955–. *W. A. Mozart: Neue Ausgabe sämtlicher Werke*. Internationale Stiftung Mozarteum Salzburg. Kassel: Bärenreiter.

Concertos

See under 'Music compositions' below.

Field recordings

Some types of investigation (such as those conducted by ethnomusicologists and anthropologists) involve making recordings of, for example, folksingers performing in their own villages or homes. This type of research is called field research, and the recordings are called field recordings. When citing such a recording it is important to include the following details:
- a description of the recording ('unaccompanied singing of the folksong "Twm, Twm y cath"');

- participants ('sung by Ben Jones, recorded by Megan Davies');
- place and date of the recording ('recorded live at the King's Arms, Felinfoel. 18 October 1998');
- also, if the recording is not your own but from an archive, you should give the name of the archive, the place where it is kept, and the catalogue number of the recording.

Instrumental works

See under 'Music compositions' below.

Jazz improvisations

In this instance you should cite either the recording (see 'CDs, records and other recordings' above), or the performance (see 'Live performances' below), or the transcription (see Chapter 7, 'Arrangements, transcriptions and editions of music'), as appropriate.

Live performances

Often, it is necessary to do no more than refer to a live performance, as in 'The British reception of American jazz was extremely enthusiastic; Miles Davis's famous concert at the Hammersmith Odeon in November 1969 attracted reviewers from all the major national newspapers.' However, if you need to refer to a live performance in a note, you should include the following details:

- the title of the piece or event;
- the names of the performers;
- the date and place of the performance.

Live performances that are recorded should be cited as recordings (see 'CDs, records and other recordings' above), but the citation should also include the date and place of the performance.

Movements in musical works

The titles of movements or major sections in musical works are usually given in roman type, with an initial capital letter but without quotes. So, for example:

The Andante of Beethoven's Sonata in E flat major, Op. 27 No. 1 opens as if it were a light divertimento.

Part Two of Ravel's *Daphnis et Chloé* makes special demands on an orchestra.

The same applies to sections of the mass:

The Gloria and the Agnus Dei were sung particularly beautifully.

Descriptive titles of movements, such as 'Roadrunner', the third movement of John Adams's *Chamber Symphony*, are given in roman type and quotes.

However, in a concert programme it is common practice to give movement titles in italics if they are foreign words.

Musical instruments

In citing musical instruments give the name and (where appropriate) the pitch of the instrument, as well as the serial number, the maker (if known) and the date of its manufacture. If the instrument is in a collection, the name of the collection and the relevant catalogue number should also be given:

Reproducing grand piano Steinway Duo-Art, Steinway & Sons, New York, 1924. National Museum 'From Musical Clock to Street Organ', Utrecht, Netherlands. Cat. no. 790.

Music arrangements

An arrangement should be cited as if it were a music composition, but the words 'arranged by' or 'arr.' followed by the name of the arranger should be added:

Beethoven's Septet in E flat major (arr. Brian Hughes)

(See also Chapter 7, 'Arrangements, transcriptions and editions of music'.)

Music compositions

There are special considerations that apply to the titles of music compositions. More than one acceptable convention exists. I have given examples of conventions for the more common types of composition – or genre – and have taken my guide from some of the leading publishers and academic journals. However, while full citations are sometimes appropriate, an intelligent shorthand for identifying works is often adequate. For example, it would be unnecessary in an article on Beethoven symphonies to give the full citation information each time a symphony is mentioned: the more common practice would be to refer, for example, to 'the Fourth Symphony'. A similar point applies to thematic catalogue numbers: you have to take a decision as to whether they are to be used or not. Usually there are good reasons for using them (although I have not used them in all my examples here). (See 'Opus numbers' and 'Thematic catalogue references' below.)

One has to distinguish between the formal title of a work and the way that the work, or part of the work, should be referred to in the flow of a text. There is no hard and fast rule for doing this, but the following general principles provide a basic framework.

- Unless you have good reasons for doing otherwise, you should spell a composer's name in the way that it is given in the main entry for that composer in *New Grove II*. So choose Stravinsky rather than Strawinski, and Tchaikovsky rather than Chaikovsky. The editors of *Grove* are fairly pragmatic in this regard, and with good reason: after all, readers will look up names and words in the spellings they are most used to.

- Where there is a descriptive title, you should give it in its most common form, for example:

  The Miraculous Mandarin, not *A csodàlatos mandarin*

  La Mer, not *The Sea*

- When the original title and the English-language equivalent are both widely used, it is best to give the original on first occurrence, followed by the translation and perhaps an explanatory note:

  Die Zauberflöte (*The Magic Flute*)

  Le Sacre du printemps (hereafter called *The Rite of Spring*)

  It follows from this that you should avoid using popular titles such as 'The Pastoral', 'The Firebird' and so on, without first providing a more formal citation.

- Use *New Grove II* to determine the opus number of a particular work (or the commonly used catalogue number – see 'Opus numbers' and 'Thematic catalogue references' below).

- As far as italics, roman and quotes are concerned, the rule of thumb is that genre titles (symphony, concerto, string quartet and so on) are normally given in roman, without quotes, while descriptive titles given to a work by the composer are given in italics, and nicknames acquired by a work are given in roman with quotes. The following list gives more detailed explanations and illustrations.

BALLETS AND OTHER CHOREOGRAPHED DANCES

Titles of complete ballets or other dance works are given in italics, as in:

Arthur Bliss, *Checkmate*

Complete acts of ballets are cited accordingly, as in:

Sleeping Beauty, Act II

The titles of named dances within ballets are given in roman and quotes, as in:

Tchaikovsky's 'Dance of the Sugar-Plum Fairy' from *The Nutcracker*

CHAMBER MUSIC

Generic titles such as String Quartet, Octet and Clarinet Quintet are given in roman, with initial capital letters, but without quotes, as in:

Beethoven's Septet in E flat major

Nicknames are given in roman and quotes, as in:

Schubert's Piano Quintet in A, 'The Trout'

CONCERTOS

The terms 'concerto' and 'concerto grosso' are generic titles, and so are normally given in roman, without quotes, as in:

Rachmaninoff's Piano Concerto No. 1

Corelli, Concerto grosso, Op. 6 No. 8

MASSES AND OTHER SACRED WORKS

When they form the names of specific religious works, words such as 'Mass' and 'Requiem' are treated as generic titles and given in roman, without quotes, and with an initial capital letter, as in:

Bach's Mass in B minor, BWV 232

Haydn's Te Deum in C, Hob. XXIIIc:1

The same pattern applies to movements within religious works (the Credo, the Sanctus and so on).

However, a religious work with a descriptive title is given in italics, as in:

Brahms's *Ein deutsches Requiem*, Op. 45

If the work has acquired a nickname, the nickname is given in roman and quotes, as in:

Mozart's 'Great' Mass in C minor, K. 427

MUSICALS

The titles of musicals are given in italics, as in:

Andrew Lloyd Webber and Tim Rice's *Evita*

Individual songs from musicals should be treated like any other song (see 'Songs and song cycles' below).

Where a musical is divided into numbered acts and scenes, and there is a need to refer to a particular scene, the act is usually given in roman and the scene in arabic numbering. So Act one, scene two would be given as: I.2. (See also Chapter 9, 'Plays'.)

OPERAS AND PARTS OF OPERAS

The titles of operas are given in italics, as in:

Puccini's *La bohème*

However, choruses, recitatives and arias, such as Rodolfo's aria 'Che gelida manina!' from that opera, are given in roman and quotes.

Where an opera is divided into numbered acts and scenes, the act should be given in roman and the scene in arabic numbering. So Act two, scene one would be given as: II.1. (See also Chapter 9, 'Plays'.)

ORATORIOS

The titles of oratorios are given in italics, as in:

Haydn's *The Creation*

OTHER INSTRUMENTAL WORKS

By 'other' instrumental works, I mean works that do not fit into one of the main genres such as concerto, sonata, symphony and so on.

Works that have descriptive titles, or that include their instrumentation in their published title, are given in italics. So, for example:

Charles Ives's *The Unanswered Question*

Bartók's *Music for Strings, Percussion and Celesta*

SONATAS

'Sonata' is a generic title and therefore normally given in roman, without quotes, as in:

Vivaldi's Sonata No. 4 in B minor, RV. 35, for violin and continuo

However, if a sonata acquires a nickname, the nickname is given in roman and quotes, as in:

Beethoven's 'Moonlight' Sonata

SONGS AND SONG CYCLES

The titles of individual songs are given in roman and quotes. Song-titles in English take capitals for all important words, unless the title forms a sentence. So:

'Rain, Rain, Beautiful Rain' (Ladysmith Black Mambazo)

but

'I will go with my father a-ploughing' (Ivor Gurney)

For song-titles in foreign languages you should usually copy the capitalization used in the source you are citing. The normal format for capitalization in modern European languages other than German is to capitalize the first word of the title and any proper nouns; in German, all nouns – common or proper – take an upper-case initial letter.

The titles of complete song cycles are given in italics, as in:

Schubert's *Die schöne Müllerin*, D. 795

SYMPHONIES

The word 'symphony' is normally taken to be a generic title and is given in roman lettering, with an initial capital letter but no quotes, as in:

Beethoven's Third Symphony

Brahms's Symphony No. 2

However, if the composer gave a descriptive title to a particular symphony, then the title is given in italics, as in:

Berlioz's *Symphonie fantastique*

If a symphony acquires a popular nickname (as opposed to a title formally given it by the composer), the nickname is given in quotes, as in:

Beethoven's Symphony No. 3 in E flat, the 'Eroica'

For symphonies by Dvořák, Mendelssohn and Schubert various numbering systems have been used. The numbering below is recommended by the journal *19th-Century Music*.

Dvořák
Symphony No. 7 in D minor, Op. 70
Symphony No. 8 in G major, Op. 88
Symphony No. 9 in E minor, Op. 95 ('From the New World')

Mendelssohn
Symphony No. 3 in A minor, Op. 56 ('Scotch' or 'Scottish')
Symphony No. 4 in A major, Op. 90 ('Italian')
Symphony No. 5 in D major, Op. 107 ('Reformation')

Schubert
Symphony No. 6 in C major, D. 589 ('Little C-major')
Symphony No. 7 in E minor, D. 729 (a sketch)
Symphony No. 8 in B minor, D. 759 ('Unfinished')
Symphony No. 9 in C major, D. 944 ('Great C-major')

The term 'chamber symphony' is not usually treated as a generic title, but rather as a descriptive name given to a work by its composer, and is therefore italicized, as in:

John Adams's *Chamber Symphony*

Music editions

As with 'Music arrangements' (see above), the normal citation should be followed by 'edited by' or 'ed.', followed by the name of the editor:

Beethoven's Septet in E flat major (ed. Brian Hughes)

(See also Chapter 7, 'Arrangements, transcriptions and editions of music'.)

work-lists in *New Grove II* if you are in doubt. See also Brook and Viano, *Thematic Catalogues in Music: An Annotated Bibliography*, cited in the bibliography below.

Catalogue numbers provide a definitive identification for a work. It is essential to use the catalogue number when there is a risk of confusion, as in:

> Mozart's Piano Concerto in E flat, K. 271, and his Piano Concerto in E flat, K. 449

Bibliography

Brook, B. S., and R. Viano, *Thematic Catalogues in Music: An Annotated Bibliography*, 2nd edn (Stuyvesant, NY: Pendragon Press, 1997).

Butcher, J., *Copy-Editing: The Cambridge Handbook for Editors, Authors and Publishers*, 3rd edn (Cambridge University Press, 1992).

The Chicago Manual of Style, 14th edn (University of Chicago Press, 1993).

Holoman, D. K., *Writing about Music: A Style Sheet from the Editors of 19th-Century Music* (Berkeley: University of California Press, 1988).

Randel, D. M. (ed.), *The New Harvard Dictionary of Music* (Cambridge, MA: Belknap Press; Harvard University Press, 1986).

Sadie, S. (ed.), *The New Grove Dictionary of Music and Musicians*, 2nd edn, 29 vols (London: Macmillan; New York: Grove's Dictionaries, 2001).

Chapter eleven

CITATIONS III: OTHER SOURCES

I N WRITINGS about music it is sometimes necessary to cite non-musical sources such as films, theatrical performances and pictures. Also, the proliferation of electronic sources (e-mail messages, on-line databases and World Wide Web sites) creates a new species of source that may need to be referred to and should be cited properly.

CD-ROMs

CD-ROMs are treated like printed texts; for citation purposes you simply identify the medium by adding 'CD-ROM' before the publication details. You should give the following information:
- author's name (if given);
- title of article or dictionary/encyclopedia entry (if you are referring to a part of the CD-ROM);
- title of CD-ROM;
- edition (if it is not the first);
- publication medium (i.e., CD-ROM);
- place of publication;
- publisher;
- date of publication.

The citation style will depend on whether you are using the short-title or author–date system (see Chapters 4 and 9).

If you are using the short-title system, the citation will read:

International Index to Music Periodicals, CD-ROM (Cambridge: Chadwyck Healey, 1996).

If you are using the author–date system, it will read:

International Index to Music Periodicals. 1996. CD-ROM. Cambridge: Chadwyck Healey.

Conversations

See 'Personal communications' below.

Films and video

Cinema films and video recordings, like radio and television broad-casts, have so many contributors that the title comes first rather than any individual's name. This is followed by the director's name (the abbreviation 'dir.' is used for 'director'), the name of the distributing company or studio and the date of the film's release:

> *Gandhi.* Dir. Richard Attenborough. Columbia. 1982.

This reference is succinct enough to give in brackets in the main body of your text. For example:

> George Fenton wrote the music for *Gandhi* (dir. Richard Attenborough. Columbia. 1982), a hugely successful film that won eight Oscars, including the 'Best Film' category of 1982.

Internet sources (e-mails, Web sites and on-line databases)

As yet, there is no general agreement on how to cite Web pages and on-line databases. However, a useful resource in this respect is Melvin Page's Guide on the H-AFRICA Web site (see the bibliography at the end of the chapter).

The content of Web sites and on-line databases is also subject to change. It can be revised and updated both easily and frequently, so if you quote from or refer to such a source the information may have been updated or removed by the time your reader tries to find it. You cannot do anything about this, of course, but you must give the date when the site or database was last revised before you took your infor-mation from it. The basic elements of a Web site reference are:

- author's name;
- name of work (if it is part of a Web site);
- name of Web site;
- URL (in angle brackets; try to fit it all on to one line);
- date of the version you are citing.

Some guidelines on the citation of e-mail sources advise you to give the author's e-mail address, but I strongly suggest (as does Page) that you should be circumspect about this as it exposes your correspondent, at least potentially, to an unknown number of unsolicited e-mails. You should not divulge any e-mail address without first asking the permission of the person whose address it is. The basic elements of an e-mail citation are:

- author's name;
- title of message;
- statement saying 'Private e-mail message';
- date when message sent.

Letters

For how to cite your own personal correspondence, see 'Personal communications' below. For unpublished correspondence between third parties, see 'Unpublished manuscripts in libraries and archives' below. For published correspondence, follow the advice on books or parts of books in Chapter 9.

Library sigla

Library sigla are convenient shorthand for citing unpublished manuscripts and their exact location. Musicologists use them frequently. Library sigla are based on a system of abbreviations. In order to understand or use this system you need to understand the abbreviation. A full list of the library sigla is published in the prefatory pages of every volume of *New Grove II*.

If you wish to cite or examine a manuscript you will need to know the library or archive where it is kept and its catalogue number. A series of letters and numbers tells you the exact location of that manuscript. Take, for example, the sigillum:

GB-Lbl Add. MS 40677

The first one or two upper-case letters tell you the country: 'GB' means Great Britain. The next upper-case letter after the hyphen tells you the town or city the archive is in, so in this case the *L* means London. The next lower-case letters give the name of the library or archive: 'bl' means The British Library. The rest of the entry is the name of the collection and/or the catalogue number in that library. Sigla for other libraries follow a similar pattern, as in:

> *F-Pn*   France, Paris, Bibliothèque Nationale
> *US-NYp*   USA, New York, Public Library

Museum exhibits and other archived objects

Each object exhibited or stored by a museum will be catalogued, and so will have a catalogue number. If you refer to such an object, you should give:

- its title (as described by the museum);
- the name of its maker, or 'anonymous';
- the place it is thought to have come from;
- the year it was made;
- the name of the museum or collection that houses it;
- the catalogue number.

For example:

> Two-manual harpsichord. Anonymous. Probably Northern Netherlands. 1658. Germanisches Nationalmuseum, Nuremberg. Inv.-Nr. MINe 84.

On-line databases

See 'Internet sources' above.

Oral interview material

There is no standardized citation method for oral interview material, but the following approach could be used. The name of the interviewee should be given. You should then use the phrase 'Interviewed by…', giving the interviewer's name (or 'the author' if you were the interviewer). You should also state whether or not the interview was recorded or broadcast. If it was broadcast, give the name of the broadcasting company or station, followed by the broadcast title and date; if not, simply give the interview date. If the oral evidence is from an archive, give the catalogue number. So, for example:

> Wulstan Atkins, E. Interviewed by the author for BBC Radio 3, *Elgar's Final Enigma.* Broadcast 15 February 1998.

Paintings and other visual art

The most important pieces of information to provide are:
* the artist's name;
* the title of the work;
* the date of the work.

Ideally, if you have it, you should also provide information about the medium of the work (the materials with which it is made), its scale (normally in centimetres, height first, followed by width), and the place and name of the collection where it is kept. Any gallery or exhibition catalogue in which the work is illustrated will provide you with this information. So, for example, if you were referring to Vermeer's painting *A Young Woman Seated at a Virginal*, you might write something like:

> People (especially young women) playing virginals are a frequent subject for seventeenth-century Dutch painters, one particularly well-known example being Vermeer's *A Young Woman Seated at a Virginal* (*c.*1670. Oil on canvas. 515 x 455 cm. London, National Gallery).

The principle is the same for sculpture and for photography.

Patents and similar formal registrations

The key items in a patent reference are:
* the name of the inventor (this may be a person, a company or an institution);
* the name or title of the registered item;
* the registration number or code;
* the registration date (if given);
* the country where registered.

For example:

> Devault, Philip J. Clarinet mechanism. Patent 527742. 1894. USA.

Personal communications

This could include conversations you have had personally or letters you have exchanged with someone else. It could also cover your own e-mail correspondence (see 'Internet sources' above). You should give the name of the person with whom you had the correspondence or the conversation, followed by the phrase 'Personal communication', and the date of the communication. For example:

> Mr Nussbaum is certain that this type of song could not have been used in Jewish religious ritual. (J. Nussbaum. Personal communication. 12 August 1999.)

Photographs

See 'Paintings and other visual art' above.

Public lectures and speeches

Give the speaker's name first, followed by the title of the speech or lecture in quotes, the place where the speech or lecture was given, and its date:

> Belshaw puts forward a persuasive argument for taking a fresh approach to musical instrument design using acoustical research as a starting point. (P. D. Belshaw. 'Acoustics and flute manufacture'. Lecture given at the Music Institute, Tenbury. 21 October 1998.)

You should not *quote* from a lecture unless you are sure that you have the exact words used by the speaker.

Radio broadcasts

See 'Television and radio broadcasts' below.

Sculptures

See 'Paintings and other visual art' above.

Tables and other data collections (published)

Tables and other data collections are usually quoted from published works. They should therefore be cited using the usual methods for citing parts of published texts (see Chapter 9) by referring to the title of the table (as given in the original source) and the page number in the publication it is taken from.

Television and radio broadcasts

Like films and videos, television and radio broadcasts involve a number of contributors, so the title comes first rather than an individual's name. This is followed by the name of the broadcasting company or station, a description of the type of programme (radio or television), unless this is obvious from the name of the company or station, and the broadcast date:

> *Big Band Special.* BBC Radio 2. 19 June 2000.

Unpublished manuscripts in libraries and archives

This category covers a wide variety of sources such as letters, diaries and other documents. Any library or archive will give each of its manuscripts a unique catalogue number, so you should take care to give the title of the collection, the name of the library or archive, and the classification mark or number of the manuscript. If it is appropriate, you could identify the library using the library sigla system (see 'Library sigla' above):

> Matthew Locke. 'Compositions for Broken and Whole consorts'.
> *GB-Lbl* Add. MS 17801 fos. 2–61.

Unpublished personal documents in private possession

If you use personal papers such as diaries and account books that are not in the public domain, they may not have a catalogue number or a library sigillum. The only solution to the problem of citation here is to use a form that is acceptable to the owner of the collection.

Bibliography

Butcher, J., *Copy-Editing: The Cambridge Handbook for Editors, Authors and Publishers*, 3rd edn (Cambridge University Press, 1992).

The Chicago Manual of Style, 14th edn (University of Chicago Press, 1993).

Dorner, J., *The Internet: A Writer's Guide* (London: A. & C. Black, 2000).

Fielden, N. L., and M. Garrido, *Internet Research: Theory and Practice* (Jefferson, N. Carolina; London: McFarland & Co., Inc., 1998).

Gibaldi, J., *MLA Handbook for Writers of Research Papers*, 4th edn (New York: The Modern Language Association of America, 1995).

MHRA Style Book, 5th edn (London: The Modern Humanities Research Association, 1996).

Page, M. E., 'A Brief Citation Guide for Internet Sources in History and the Humanities', H-AFRICA Web site, at: <http://www2.h-net.msu.edu/~africa/citation.html> 20 February 1996.

GLOSSARY

This glossary is intended to help you find your way to relevant sections of the book. It is not intended to be comprehensive (it does not, for example, list musical terms). (For more detailed directions, use the Index.)

academic journals periodical publications, often issued by learned societies. A journal is usually dedicated to one particular aspect of a broader subject, or the interests of a particular society (for example, there are music journals with the titles *19th-Century Music*, *Early Music*, the *Historic Brass Society Journal* and so on). Journals contain scholarly articles and reviews of the latest books or recordings relevant to the subject of the journal.

adjective put simply, a word that adds more information about a noun (e.g., a *large* box; she is *tall* for her age; an *old* man).

advanced search a search performed on an electronic library catalogue or **search engine** which allows you to specify the terms you want to find, and eliminate terms you don't want. (See Chapter 3.)

ampersand the symbol '&'.

anachronism an idea, object, person or event which is outside its proper historical period.

angle brackets < > used in written text to mark off e-mail and Web site addresses from the words that surround them. (See Chapter 6.)

annex a supplement to the main text, containing illustrations, for example.

appendix (appendices) like an **annex**, a supplement to the main text.

arabic numbering figures (1, 2, 3, 4, 5 and so on) are used rather than letters (see also **roman numbering** below, and Chapter 6).

Aslib the Association for Information Management, based in London.

author–date system one of the two main citation methods for written texts. (See Chapters 4 and 9.)

bibliography a list of books and other written texts. (See Chapter 4.)

bookmarks an option on your browser screen that allows you to assemble a collection of the addresses of your most frequently used Web sites, for easy access (sometimes also called 'Favourites').

Boolean search kind of search of an electronic database, such as a library catalogue, using 'Boolean operators' (the words 'and', 'or' and 'not'). Named after George Boole (1815–64). (See Chapter 3.)

CD-ROM stands for Compact Disk – Read Only Memory. Similar to an audio CD, but can hold large quantities of visual and textual data as well as sound.

citation convention a systematic and commonly understood way of giving the details of a source you have used, so as to enable your readers to find the source for themselves. (See Chapters 4, 9–11.)

clause a group of words containing a finite verb (see **verb** below and Chapter 6, 'Sentences').

colloquialism a word or phrase that derives from informal, spoken language (for example, the expression 'to scrap [something]', as in: 'They were going to play an encore but decided to scrap it.').

compound word a term made up of two or more words (either **nouns** or **adjectives**), which may or may not be hyphenated. For instance, 'brass band' is a compound noun. Many compound nouns do not need to be hyphenated. However, 'silver-plated' is a compound adjective, and these usually do require a hyphen. (See Chapter 6.)

copyright page the **verso** of the **title page** of a published book; it gives the book's copyright details and **International Standard Book Number**. (See Chapter 4.)

discography a list of recordings. (See Chapter 4.)

displayed quotation a quotation (usually more than three lines long) that is set apart from the main body of the text, usually by indenting it and/or setting it in a different **font** size from the main text. (See Chapter 6, 'Quotations'.)

double spacing a word-processor setting that allows you to leave a gap of one line between each line of typed text.

download to transfer data (for example, from a **Web site**) to your own computer.

finite verb see **verb**.

foliation the numbering of the folios (see below) in a manuscript.

folio both sides of a **leaf** in a manuscript. (Compare with **page** below.)

font (also 'fount') – a set of type of the same size and style.

full-text search a search that allows you to find every occurrence of a particular **keyword** or phrase in an electronic text or database.

homepage the opening page of a **World Wide Web** site.

house style the writing and formatting style (including particular rules for spelling, use of capital letters, the look and layout of the page) used by a publisher. House styles differ from publisher to publisher.

humanities the academic disciplines (such as history, literature, philosophy, art history, music and so on) that are concerned with the study of human culture.

hypertext highlighted words or phrases that act as links from one Web document or page to another when you click on them with the mouse button.

indent to start a line further in than the standard page margin.

International Standard Book Number (ISBN) unique identifying number ascribed to every book published since 1970.

International Standard Serial Number (ISSN) unique identifying number ascribed to **periodical** publications such as **academic journals** and magazines.

Internet an electronic network connecting computers throughout the world so as to exchange information via text, sound and images.

italics letters that slope to the right, *like this.*

keyword a significant word that can be used to identify a work, person or topic in, for example, a database search.

leaf a single sheet of paper in a book or manuscript.

lower case 'small' letters – that is, letters that are not capital letters (compare with **upper case**).

metasearch engine a fast, powerful type of **search engine** that gets results by searching a number of other search engines.

microfiche a means of storing written or graphical information by reducing its size and printing it on a single flat (postcard-size) sheet of cellophane, which is read using a special machine called a 'micro-fiche reader'.

microfilm a similar process to **micro-fiche**, but the data is stored on a reel of film. Like microfiche, it is read using a special machine called a 'microfilm reader'.

monograph a piece of academic writing about a single subject or aspect of a subject.

multimedia a term describing electronic, **on-line** sources that use combinations of written text, graphics, sound, photographs, video and so on.

noun often described as a 'naming word'. Nouns cover a huge range: proper nouns (e.g., John, Australia, Hong Kong); common nouns

(e.g., box, instrument); abstract nouns (e.g., anger, happiness); collective nouns (e.g., people, group).

object in a sentence, the thing to which an action is done. For example, in the sentence 'They sang the chorus', the object is 'the chorus'. (See also **subject** below and Chapter 6, 'Sentences'.)

on-line available through an **Internet** connection.

opening literally, what you see when you open a book at any point: the two pages on either side of the spine.

page one side of a **leaf** in a book or journal. (Compare with **folio** above.)

pagination the numbering of the **pages** of a book or journal.

paraphrasing taking someone else's ideas and expressing them in your own words. (See Chapter 4.)

periodical a publication that is issued *periodically* (every day, weekly, monthly, several times a year and so on), such as a newspaper or **academic journal**.

portal a **Web site** that provides a compendium of links to other sites.

prefatory material the material that precedes the main content of a book (the contents, acknowledge-ments page and so on).

prefix a group of letters such as un-, re- or anti-, added to a word to alter its meaning in some way (e.g., doing, *un*doing, *re*doing).

primary source any text, object, image or recorded sound that can be used as the essential raw material for research. A primary source is one that originated in the period of a given topic. (See also **secondary source** below.)

prior explanations a list of explanations of special abbreviations and other conventions that are used in a piece of writing.

process words words in an essay question such as 'discuss', 'explain' and 'consider' that define the precise nature of the task that has been set. (See Chapter 1.)

pronoun may be used instead of a noun (e.g., I, you, he, she, it, one, we, they).

quotation material by another writer or a composer which you reproduce in your own writing. A 'quotation' is not the same as a 'quote' – see **quotes** below. (See also **displayed quotation** above, and Chapter 6, 'Quotations' and 'Quotation marks'.)

quotes another term for 'quotation marks'. Material that you quote should be referred to as a 'quotation', not a 'quote'. (See Chapter 6, 'Quotations' and 'Quotation marks'.)

recto a right-hand page in a book, or the front side of a leaf. (See also **leaf** and **verso**.)

reference another term for a citation (see **citation convention**). Also used in the sense of a *reference book* – that is, a book that provides factual information (e.g. dictionaries are reference books).

research and reference tools reference sources that contain bibliographies and other elements that identify sources relevant to a topic.

roman type that is not in **italics** (e.g. this is roman – *this is italics*).

roman numbering letters (i, ii, iii, iv, v and so on) are used instead of figures (see also **arabic numbering** above, and Chapter 6).

scholarly conventions the procedures of formal academic writing (including forms of **citation convention** – see above).

search engine a free **Web site**, such as Alta Vista or Yahoo!, which allows you to find other Web sites by using **keywords**. (See also **metasearch engine** above.)

secondary source a book, article and so on that comments on or analyses a theme or topic for which a **primary source** is used as evidence, or other source material that, because it was created after the period under investigation, has a lower status than a primary source.

short-title system one of the two main citation systems for written texts. (See Chapters 4 and 9.)

source any writing, recording or physical object (such as an instrument) that is studied in a research project. (See also **primary source** and **secondary source** above, and Chapter 2.)

style manual a reference book that explains the standard rules about formal, academic writing.

subject the subject of a sentence is who or what the sentence is about. For example, in the sentence 'She played the violin' the subject is 'she'. (See also **object** above and Chapter 6, 'Sentences'.)

subject keyword (searches) a way of searching computerized catalogues. (See **keyword** above and Chapter 3.)

subscript a type character printed below the line: this is in subscript

superscript a type character printed above the line (used to signal footnotes, for example): this is in superscript

tense the tense of a **verb** shows *when* an action, feeling or process happens. On the simplest level, things happen in the *past*, the *present* or the *future*: ('He *played* the flute' (past)/'He *plays* the flute' (present)/'He *will play* the flute' (future)). However, the relationship of tenses to time is rather more complex than this basic view would suggest. (See Chapter 6, 'Tenses'.)

title page the page of a book or work of music that carries the title, the name of the author or composer (and arranger if there is one), and the publisher's details. (See Chapter 4.)

upper case capital letters: THIS IS UPPER CASE.

URL Uniform Resource Locator. Simply, a **World Wide Web** address (for example, <http://www.abrsmpublishing.co.uk>).

verb expresses an action or a condition ('He *seems* very nice'; 'she *played* the violin'; 'It *rained*' etc.). A finite verb is the verb together with its **subject** ('He seems', 'she played', 'it rained'). You cannot have a sentence without a finite verb.

verso a left-hand page in a book, or the back of a leaf. (See also **leaf** and **recto**.)

Web see **World Wide Web** below.

Web site a part of the **World Wide Web** with a unique **URL**. Web sites can have many pages.

wildcard a device used in computer catalogue searches. (See Chapter 3.)

World Wide Web a user-friendly way of navigating through the massive collection of information sites carried by the **Internet**.

INDEX

This index includes terms that are dealt with in the book and some that are not: various alternative words (dance/ballet, full stop/period and so on) are given in order to make it possible to find topics by more than one route. Concise definitions of many non-musical terms are given in the Glossary, which starts on page 203. Glossary entries are not included in this index.